MAGDALEN COLLEGE SCHOOL

Laurence Brockliss

SHIRE PUBLICATIONS

Published in Great Britain in 2016 by Shire Publications Ltd (part of Bloomsbury Publishing Plc), PO Box 883, Oxford, OX1 9PL, UK.

PO Box 3985, New York, NY 10185-3985, USA.

E-mail: shire@shirebooks.co.uk
www.shirebooks.co.uk

A CIP catalogue record for this book is available from the British Library.

ISBN-13: 978 1 78442 151 9
PDF: 978 1 78442 153 3
EPub: 978 1 78442 152 6

Editor: Ruth Sheppard

Indexer: Mark Swift

Page design by Stewart Larking and typeset in Perpetua.

Printed in China through World Print Ltd.

16 17 18 19 20   10 9 8 7 6 5 4 3 2 1

COVER IMAGE
May Day celebrations on Magdalen Tower. Sydney Prior Hall, wood engraving with tone-plate, 1885.

BACK COVER IMAGE
Madrigals, 2000. A twentieth-century innovation, madrigals are one of the most popular events of the MCS year.

TITLE PAGE IMAGE
Variant on a well-worn theme: the daily chorister procession from the School to the College chapel is a well-known Oxford routine. Here, the iteration is not quite so stately.

CONTENTS PAGE IMAGE
School Field in winter.

PHOTOGRAPH ACKNOWLEDGEMENTS
Images reproduced by kind permission of:
the President and Fellows of Magdalen College, Oxford, pages 15, 24, 35, 47, 70 (top); the National Portrait Gallery, page 19; the Church Commissioners, page 31; © Birmingham Museums Trust, page 46; the Master, Fellows and Scholars of the College of St Peter le Bailey in the University of Oxford, page 50; the Warden and Fellows of All Souls College, Oxford, page 56; the collection of Michael and Clova Stinton, page 59; and *The Oxford Mail*, page 71 (top).

All other photographs are from the archives of Magdalen College School, Oxford. Archive photography by John Gibbons.

Shire Publications is supporting the Woodland Trust, the UK's leading woodland conservation charity, by funding the dedication of trees.

CONTENTS

INTRODUCTION

MAGDALEN COLLEGE SCHOOL Oxford was established in 1480 by William Waynflete, Bishop of Winchester, as part of his larger foundation of Magdalen College. Now well over 500 years old, it has had a long and chequered history. In the first years of its existence, it was an innovatory and highly regarded Latin school, attracting pupils from around the country. From the mid-sixteenth century, however, it lost its innovative edge, and for the next 300 years it was simply one of England's many small-town grammar schools serving the educational needs of the local community. Its fortunes only began to look up after 1870 under a series of effective Masters who developed a boarding department, expanded the curriculum, and improved its facilities. Since then MCS has never looked back and today is firmly established as one of the country's leading independent schools. Its present status has not been achieved without considerable effort. In the twentieth century, it moved from being a private grammar school under the control of the College to a school largely maintained by the local authority, then back once more to being an independent school but now with its own governing body. With no endowment to speak of, every change to its status and every improvement in its facilities was only effected after much debate and soul-searching. MCS's present position owes everything to the old members, parents, and more recently governors who dedicated their time and often their money to turning a modest school into a great one.

The present history offers a brief account of the School over the past 530 years. It is intended to complement but not replace the two earlier histories of MCS written by Robert Stanier, Master 1944–67, and Denis Clark. Stanier's *Magdalen School: A History of Magdalen College School Oxford* was published in 1958, the year the College celebrated its 500th anniversary. Clark's *Magdalen School: 500 Years On* was published in 1980 and took the story up to the School's own quincentenary. The first ended with MCS as a direct-grant grammar school, the second at the start of the School's return to the private sector. This history takes the narrative up to 2007 and the

Opposite:
Aerial view, with MCS in the foreground, after the opening of the New Building in 2008.

5

departure of Andrew Halls, Master from 1998, who along with his predecessor, Peter Tinniswood, laid the foundations of today's success. Since 1980 there has been only one substantial contribution to the history of MCS. In 1998, Professor Nicholas Orme, a medieval historian of education, published *Education in Early Tudor England: Magdalen College and its School, 1480–1540*, a detailed account of MCS's early history when it pioneered a new approach to teaching Latin.

The text of this brief account began life as a series of sections to *Magdalen College: A History*, a volume published for the College in 2008 to mark its 550th anniversary. As the College has had three schools under its control for most of its existence, it was felt that their history had to be depicted alongside the College's own. The intention was not to describe life at MCS, still less details such as sports results and concert programmes. Rather, the interest was in the relationship between the College and the School and how far changes in the College affected the school provision. This history then is an account of a relationship between a parent and its child, with all the inevitable tiffs and reconciliations, and how the child finally became an independent adult. As editor of the College history, I am indebted to my deputy editor, Andrew Hegarty, the College archivist, Robin Darwall-Smith, and the Fellow Librarian, Christine Ferdinand, for their help in reconstructing the history of the School from the College archives. In the case of the present account, the Master, Dr Tim Hands, and I would like to thank Ruth Sheppard for turning the individual sections from the College history into a readable narrative, and thank Sarah Broadway, Matthew Clifford, Lucy Hambidge and Meg Weissmann for their help in seeing the book through the press.

A complete up-to-date history of MCS still has to be written. The present account can at best be a taster to whet the appetite. It is hoped that the reader will find the narrative informative and engaging, and that he or she will be convinced by the end that a good school like a good life is the product of relentless hard work.

Laurence Brockliss
21 January 2016

CRoberti whittyntoni lichfeldiēcis grā
matices magistri ⁊ prothouatis Anglie in
floꝛētissima Oꝛoniēsi achademia laurea
ti. Editio de concinnitate grammatices ⁊
constructione.

THE GRAMMAR SCHOOL AND THE NEW LEARNING: 1480–1688

MAGDALEN COLLEGE WAS founded in 1458 by William Waynflete, Bishop of Winchester and Lord Chancellor. In 1480, the new President Richard Mayhew implemented the lengthy and detailed statutes drawn up by the Founder, including his requirement that the endowment support a grammar school on the College site which would offer free education. William Waynflete's foundation of a grammar school at the College was probably influenced by the time he had spent teaching at Winchester and Eton. His first proper position had been as Magister Informator, effectively the head teacher of grammar, at Winchester College, which was founded in the late fourteenth century by Bishop William of Wykeham. In 1441, Henry VI visited Winchester College, and soon afterwards Waynflete was teacher of Latin grammar at Henry's school, Eton. There Waynflete's abilities became apparent, and after two years he was promoted to be provost. While Henry busied himself in securing papal privileges for Eton and planning the erection of its quadrangle and a chapel of cathedral dimensions, Waynflete was able to lay its sound educational foundations, expanding the entry of twenty-five boys in 1444 to the full complement of seventy by 1447. When, after Waynflete's retirement from the provostship, Henry drew up his will in February 1448, setting out his plan for the twin foundations at Eton and Cambridge, it was to Waynflete that he entrusted its supervision and execution.

Waynflete's school at Magdalen was to be a very different school from those set up by William of Wykeham and Henry VI. It had no separate endowment, nor was it a feeder school like the other two; its pupils had no right to expect an eventual place on the College Foundation. The grammar school was to be a public institution, for its doors were to be open 'to all persons whomsoever', not just the sixteen boy choristers of the College Choir and younger demies (scholars at the College). By implication, then, it was to be a school for boys from the town as well as scholars in the University, and it was clearly intended to prop up the declining provision of

Opposite: Woodcut from *Whittintoni Opuscula de Concinnita Gramma*, a Latin grammar book published by Robert Whittinton, Old Boy of the School, in 1518. The illustration depicts a contemporary teacher with his pupils, a scene doubtless echoed at Magdalen College School.

9

Portrait of Bishop William Waynflete, founder of Magdalen College and Magdalen College School, from Richard Chandler's *Life of William Waynflete*, 1811.

Opposite: A less idealised and anonymous portrayal of Waynflete. Oil on canvas, probably seventeenth century.

grammar teaching in Oxford. Boys were to be admitted by an examination held once a year on 21 July, the eve of St Mary Magdalen day. The Master and Usher (assistant master) were to be members of the Foundation, with their stipends and the maintenance of the schoolroom being a direct charge upon College revenues. The two teachers were to be paid annual salaries of £10 and £5 respectively, with commons in College at the same rate as Fellows, and free lodgings.

The School appears to have opened at Easter 1480 in an old building within the College curtilage to the south of the chapel.[1] It occupied a vaulted chamber below the old chapel of St John's Hospital, which was joined up with the Tower in 1508/9. The building, however, was unsuitable for a classroom – it was cold, and about 2 feet below ground level. Unsurprisingly, the School was soon moved beyond the entrance courtyard to a purpose-built schoolroom begun in the autumn of the same year.

The new building, which would house the School until the mid-nineteenth century, when it was transferred to what is now the New Library, was situated to the west of the entrance courtyard, later to be known as St John's Quadrangle. It was a two-storey building in the late perpendicular style measuring about 70 feet by 24 feet, lying north–south. Its entrance fronted onto, but was set back from, the main thoroughfare leading from the city's east gate to the bridge so that the view from the College's outer main gate to the city's walls along what was to become known as the Gravel Walk was not obscured. The roof was pitched and tiled with two chimneys, while a turret on the north-east corner gave access to the leads. The ground floor was used as a schoolroom, and the upper floor as living accommodation for the Master and Usher. Later in the sixteenth century the upper floor was remodelled to contain a chapel at the south end for the use of the inhabitants of neighbouring Magdalen Hall, and later still an attic floor was added.[2] The building had approximately the same dimensions as both the schoolroom at Eton, and the one at Wainfleet, which Waynflete had founded in 1466. The schoolroom had space for about a hundred pupils and was lit by windows placed high in the walls to discourage distraction from without. The Master and Usher would have sat at either end, the Usher near the door, while the pupils occupied benches or forms set sideways-on and running the length of the room. It can

Previous pages:
Magdalen College
School as seen
from the Gravel
Walk. In reality,
the east façade
would have been
obscured by the
wall between
the School and
the College
and the College's
main gate. Etching
with engraving,
anonymous,
c. 1800.

be assumed that eventually, if not initially, boys were grouped according to levels of attainment. The School was separated physically from the College by a passageway, but there appears to have been a wicket gate in the east wall which allowed access to the College's entrance courtyard.

The Founder intended the School to offer free tuition in grammar to all comers, town and gown alike, and not only to choristers and younger demies.[3] It was presumably for this reason that the School was located outside the inner curtilage, so that young boys in need of instruction in Latin, whether or not they were members of the University, might receive tuition without entering the College proper. The School's separation from the College also ensured that pupils would not mix with or be disturbed by older students attending lectures or on other business. The school day was long – from 5.00 a.m. to 5.00 p.m. with breaks for breakfast and lunch – and keeping young noses constantly to the grindstone must have been difficult. Even in a separate building, discipline does not seem to have been easy to maintain, and recourse to the birch (the favourite English instrument of chastisement) was commonplace.[4]

Next to nothing definite is known about the pattern of attendance in the first centuries of the School's existence, but there can be no doubt that it quickly attracted outsiders. In part, this was probably because it lacked direct competitors. In the fourteenth and the first part of the fifteenth centuries, Oxford had been an important centre of grammar teaching and possibly half a dozen academic halls offered instruction in the subject for a fee. By 1470, however, most, if not all, of these schools had shut, so there was nowhere else in the city for scholars to go for such public instruction. Waynflete's foundation, therefore, filled a gap, which possibly explains why he had decided to attach a grammar school to the College in the first place.[5] Chiefly, however, pupils flocked to the School because of the quality of its teaching.

Detailed information about the nature of grammar teaching at individual institutions in fifteenth- and sixteenth-century England is usually unobtainable, but enough is known about the teaching of Magdalen's first Master, John Anwykyll, to understand why the School so quickly gained such a high reputation. Anwykyll was a Cambridge man who seems to have been purposely brought to Oxford by Waynflete. He is first mentioned in the College archives as Master in 1483/4, in which year he quite likely published at Oxford a compendium of grammar, possibly at the Founder's behest.[6] There is nothing particularly innovative about the pedagogical techniques espoused in the work. The introduction of basic grammatical points through a question and answer format, their illustration in specimen Latin sentences, and the use of mnemonic verses to ram the lesson home were all devices developed by earlier grammarians, notably John Leland,

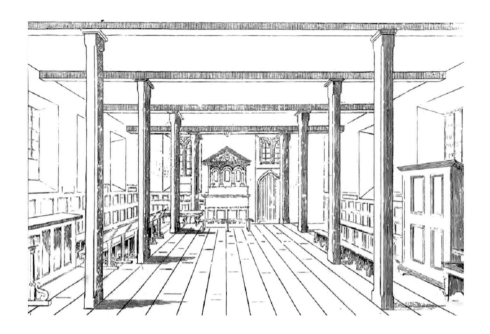

The original
schoolroom,
1828 engraving.

who had been the leading Oxford schoolmaster of the early fifteenth century.[7] Anwykyll's originality lay rather in his championship of the new style of more classical Latin being promoted in Renaissance Italy. His illustrative sentences were not usually of his own contrivance but drawn from approved classical authors, particularly the playwright Terence. He also gave his charges English translations of Terence to render back into Latin.[8] Whether Anwykyll and his pupils were also reading complete classical texts in class remains unknown, but he clearly wanted boys to emerge from the School writing and speaking the Latin of Cicero rather than that of Duns Scotus and his late-medieval followers.

Anwykyll died in 1487, shortly after the College had demonstrated its contentment with his teaching in previous years by offering him a fifteen-year contract. During that time, he was to 'read and teach grammar, poetry, refinements of speech (*elegantia*) and other apt humanities'.[9] His enthusiasm for the new Latin was shared by his immediate successors as Master: John Stanbridge (1488–93/94); Andrew Scarbott (1494–99); the young Thomas Wolsey (Easter to Michaelmas 1499); Richard Jackson (1499–1501); and Thomas Brinknell (1502–07), who had earlier run the school at Wainfleet.[10] Of these, the most famous grammarian nationally was Stanbridge, an Oxford MA who had been educated at Winchester and New College, and became Usher in 1486. He seems to have left the School after five years to

A grammarian, maybe early Master John Stanbridge himself, birch in hand, giving a Latin lesson. The print appears in Stanbridge's own Latin grammar book, *Vocabula Magistri Stanbrigi Sua Saltem Editione Edita*, published in 1523.

teach grammar to novices at the Abbey of Winchcombe, then moved again to take over a school at Lichfield, before finally becoming Master of the Hospital of St John at Banbury, Oxfordshire, in 1501. There he established a grammar school, where he taught the new Latin until his death in 1510.[11] Stanbridge was, therefore, a schoolmaster for some twenty-five years. While at Magdalen he published nothing, but in the last five years of his life he put a complete set of grammatical texts into the public domain, starting with his *Accidence* of 1505, which was thereafter reprinted repeatedly for thirty years.[12]

As no other grammar school in England is known to have taught the new humanist Latin in 1480, Magdalen inevitably commanded the market.[13] As the new learning gained increasing respectability at court, astute fathers and patrons all round the country must have seen the wisdom of sending their sons and clients to the College School to improve their chances of preferment. Although there has been an erroneous tendency over the years to assume that every English humanist and high-flying ecclesiastic of the first decades of the sixteenth century must have passed through its portals, there can be no doubt that several did so. Bishop Longland of Lincoln and Archbishop Lee of York were certainly pupils. So too was William Tyndale, translator of the Bible.[14] Two other school alumni became leading humanist grammarians – William Lily and Robert Whittin(g)ton. Lily (demy 1486) later travelled in the Holy Land and studied in Italy before returning to London and becoming the first High Master of Dean Colet's reconstituted St Paul's School in 1509. In 1515 Lily published an important co-authored grammar, the same year in which he was joined at St Paul's by a former Usher of the School, Maurice Birchynshaw.[15] Whittinton, a pupil of Stanbridge, was a schoolmaster in the first decade of the sixteenth century, and then spent the second publishing a number of grammatical textbooks whose appeal would prove even greater than those of his Master. In the 1530s and 1540s he went on to translate Cicero and Seneca into English.[16]

If the numbers who attended the College School from outside the city in these early years were really as large as tradition claims, then cramming these grammarians into the existing halls and colleges must have been a problem. It is possibly for this reason that a new hall was established on Magdalen land towards the end of the fifteenth century, directly to the west of the School, in a building that fronted the main thoroughfare. That said, it must be stressed that the origins of Magdalen Hall, which came to occupy much of the site of the modern St Swithun's Quad, are shrouded in mystery. All that is known is that by the end of the century the College had erected or restored a building at right angles to the School, which fronted the later Gravel Walk. This was extended further west in 1518. By the early 1490s, if not before, this building was leased to one of the College Fellows at a peppercorn rent, and the Fellow in question was called the principal of

THOMAS WOLSEY Arch-Bíſhop *of Yorke* , Chancelovr *of England* Cardinal *and* Legate *de* Latere. He Died at Leiceſter Abby *Anno* Dñi 1529. *the* 29th *of November* . W.M. ſculp.

Cardinal Thomas Wolsey, probably a pupil, and later briefly Master of the School. Engraving by William Marshall after T. Fuller, 1642. Illustration to Thomas Fuller, *The Holy State* (Cambridge, R. D. for John Williams, 1642).

17

Magdalen Hall. Like any other hall principal, he in turn rented rooms to scholars for profit and was responsible for maintaining good discipline.[17]

Whatever the truth of the matter, Magdalen Hall could never have developed in the way that it was to do in the second half of the sixteenth and early seventeenth centuries had it relied on grammarians only. The College School's glory days lasted less than thirty years. After 1560, by contrast, Magdalen Hall entered its golden age. In 1579 there were probably about sixty scholars on its books, but by 1624 there were purportedly 300, forty of whom were MAs. Over the period as a whole, the same number of students matriculated from College and Hall. Indeed, although the number of matriculands from the Hall appear to have declined sharply after 1660, on paper it was the more populous institution before the Civil War. In the 1600s the Hall supplied the fifth largest number of matriculands in the University, in the 1630s the second. Not surprisingly, Magdalen Hall was the Oxford institution of many statesmen, clerics and writers of the period, most notably the philosopher Thomas Hobbes, a clergyman's son, who matriculated from it in 1603. Moreover, although a hall, its undergraduate tenants were not excluded from the burgeoning tutorial system: its matriculands were either placed under the care of resident MAs or looked after by outside tutors.

Inevitably, in the wake of the College School's success, new grammar schools were established and old ones, such as St Paul's, refounded, in which the new Latin was taught equally well. Often, as at St Paul's, former teachers and pupils of Magdalen's school were involved in the process, but the notion of a diaspora should not be exaggerated. No one who had attended the School is known ever to have been employed at Winchester. Rival schools began to appear even in Oxford, temporarily.[18] Increasingly, then, many potential pupils were lured away to their local schools and Magdalen College School, Oxford, lost much of its *élan*.

Opposite: Woodcut illustration depicting the execution by strangulation and burning of former pupil William Tyndale. From John Foxe's *Acts and Monuments*, published 1563, better known as Foxe's 'Book of Martyrs'. Tyndale, a Protestant agitator, was the first scholar to translate the Latin Bible into English vernacular.

Seventeenth-century line engraving of William Lily, grammarian and alumnus. Author of a famous Latin grammar primer that became known as 'Lily's Grammar', the industry standard for centuries.

This is not to say that the quality of the teaching at the School declined in the first half of the sixteenth century, for a number of Masters and Ushers were figures of consequence: notably, Thomas Robertson (Master 1526–34) and Thomas Cooper (Master 1549–57 and 1558–67). The former was another important humanist grammarian and Dean of Durham under Mary, and the latter, son of a poor Oxford tailor, successively Bishop of Lincoln and then Winchester under Elizabeth, as well as the author of a famous English and Latin dictionary.[19] The School, moreover, continued to attract high achievers. Robertson's pupils included John Parkhurst, Elizabethan Bishop of Norwich; and the leading Elizabethan antiquarian and Headmaster of Westminster School, William Camden, author of the topographical classic, *Britannia* (1586). Neither came from Oxford, so both seem to have been sent to the School while young boys as the result of a deliberate choice.[20]

It is impossible to assess what intellectual effect the humanist school had on the College's Fellowship. As a significant proportion of the demies became Fellows and many of them would have spent time in the School, it can perhaps be assumed that the Fellowship was not uninfluenced by the new learning.[21] However, it should not be concluded that College praelectors, or lecturers, would in consequence have come to offer a humanist rather than a scholastic exegesis of traditional set texts. By the mid-sixteenth century most scholars throughout Europe were trained in the new Latin, but this did little to undermine the traditional scholastic approach to philosophy and theology. Despite the hostility of Erasmus to scholastic learning, the old and the new soon found a *modus vivendi*.[22] As it is, virtually nothing is known about the content of College teaching before the eighteenth century, so the exact degree of humanist influence will never be known.

It would, however, be surprising if that influence had been dramatic. The very fact that in 1517 Richard Fox, Bishop of Winchester, instructed the foundationers of Corpus to take their scholastic instruction at Magdalen would suggest that Magdalen praelectors offered standard fare.[23] At this time Magdalen had three praelectors, one in theology, another in natural philosophy and a third in ethics and metaphysics. The lectures were free of charge and open to all. Indeed, the only evidence that the praelectors of Magdalen might have promoted the new learning at any time in the period lies in the fact that the first Praelector of Theology was the ardent humanist, William Grocyn, who held the post from 1483 to 1488. A Fellow of New College, Grocyn eventually gave up his Magdalen post to travel to Italy, whence he returned to teach Greek for a time in the University's Schools.[24] As he appears to have known the language in some degree before his appointment at Magdalen, it seems unlikely that he taught theology wholly in the traditional manner. None

Opposite:
William Camden, antiquarian and author of *Britannia*, a pupil in the 1560s. Oil on canvas, probably early seventeenth century.

the less, he would surely have had to provide his pupils with the skills they would need to take part in public disputations, and cannot, therefore, have deviated greatly from the common line.

The College's more general commitment to the new learning, furthermore, should certainly not be exaggerated. If it had been, Fox would presumably not have needed to found Corpus Christi College, nor Wolsey Cardinal College (the future Christ Church) a few years later, where the deeper study of the humanities was to be given rather more substantial encouragement.[25] Although President John Claymond was something of a humanist, and several Magdalen Fellows were cherry-picked by Bishop Fox and Cardinal Thomas Wolsey to adorn their new humanistic foundations, hardly any Fellow in the period 1480–1560 was to make a contribution to humanist exegesis in the novel medium of print.[26] Significantly, too, of the fifty or so men who were Masters or Ushers of the School during these years, only Scarbott, Wolsey, Jackson and John Stokesley were resident Fellows. Moreover, although the stipend was competitive, only one ex-Fellow, Thomas Cooper, became Master of the School later in life, and he came from a particularly lowly background.[27] Fellows were clearly not entranced by the prospect of teaching the new Latin.

It is surely significant, too, that despite its theological emphasis, Magdalen was slow to use its wealth to encourage study of the original languages of scripture, knowledge of which was essential in the eyes of Erasmus and other leading humanists of northern Europe, if Christianity was to be renewed. The School taught its pupils to read, write and speak classical Latin. There is no evidence in this period that it ever taught Greek, let alone Hebrew, Syriac or Aramaic. Before 1536, moreover, there is no evidence that the College itself offered tuition in these languages. A Greek praelectorship came into existence only because it was officially instituted by Thomas Cromwell's Visitors in 1535, at which time Latin and Greek lectures were also established in other colleges by government fiat:

> Pleasit your goodnes to be advertisyde that in Magdalen College we fownde stablishede one Lecture of Divinitie, two of Philosophie – one Morale, another Naturale – and one of Latin tonge [the School], well kept and diligently frequentede. To this we have adjonede a Lecture in the Greke, that is, the Grammar in Greke perpetually to be rede there, and all the yewthe therunto to have confluence for their principulles.[28]

In other words Magdalen, like other Oxford colleges founded before 1500, was no humanist powerhouse in the early Tudor era. Before the mid-1530s, if demies and Fellows wanted to become Hellenists or Hebraists, they would have had either to learn these languages on their own, go abroad, seek a private tutor, or, from the 1520s onwards, go to another college.[29] Through its school Magdalen may have aided the dissemination of a new style of Latin in England, but it played little part in promoting humanist learning in any wider sense.

In the late sixteenth and seventeenth centuries, the School was no longer the beacon of humanist education it had once been. It was served by a series of competent Masters and Ushers for most of the period, but none were national celebrities, and only the puritanical John Harmar (demy 1610–17; Usher 1617–26), published a textbook, *Praxis Grammatica* (1623).[30] By then, moreover, few boys attended the School who were not on the Foundation or natives of Oxford: there was no longer a national clientele. It would be rash, however, to dismiss the School as moribund. Even with its limited recruitment base, it still educated a number of distinguished churchmen and men of letters during the period. College Presidents Accepted Frewen and Thomas Pierce were alumni, as were William Nicholson, a future Bishop of Gloucester, Henry Holyoake, reforming Headmaster of Rugby, and the poet, Thomas Yalden, who entered the School as choristers in 1589, 1672 and 1678 respectively.[31]

Nor was the School neglected by the College. The College President Laurence Humphrey was reprimanded by the Visitor in 1585 for allowing it to decay under William Symonds (demy 1573; Fellow 1578–83, Master 1583–86),[32] but generally the College fulfilled its responsibilities and the two institutions lived in easy coexistence throughout the period. The Master and Usher were always part of the Foundation, and from the Restoration, if not before, the former doubled as College Praelector in Greek.[33] In this regard the Oxford school was treated more benignly than the two other grammar schools in the College's care, Wainfleet (founded 1459) and Brackley (founded 1548).

THE QUIET YEARS: 1688–1854

FOLLOWING THE RESTORATION, Oxford and Cambridge Universities entered a quiet phase that would last until the reforms of the mid-eighteenth century. The history of the School during these years reflects the wider fortunes of Oxford.

While some of the School's teachers during the eighteenth and nineteenth century, such as Thomas Collins (Master 1673–1723), and Edward Ellerton (Usher 1795–98 and Master 1798–1810), were figures of some consequence in their own right, the School did not reflect this significance.[1] Some appointees, indeed, did nothing for its standards. Under George Grantham (Usher 1801–40; Fellow 1809–40), the School seems to have virtually collapsed. Grantham was a drunkard, who eventually died by falling from his window into the Grove while intoxicated. Even the discreet John Bloxam (demy 1830–35, Fellow 1835–63, and biographer of many at the College) had to admit: 'I have been told by persons most likely to know the facts, that in the management of his pupils he studied his own convenience rather than their improvement'.[2]

Others corroborated this picture of a neglected school. James E. Millard (Master 1846–64) reminisced in 1881 about his schooldays in the 1830s:

> We were so entirely uncontrolled – so completely a law unto ourselves that the evil compelled a remedy from within. Like settlers in San Francisco, we could only maintain even our approach to morality or discipline by organising 'vigilance committees', and taking the (lynch) law into our own hands. We used to form an oligarchy of 'four seniors' (I hardly know how chosen) who were very arbitrary and severe, and upon the whole exercised a tolerably wholesome influence.[3]

Millard became one of several Masters who improved standards at the School in the 1840s and 1850s. A visible sign of this improvement was the erection of a brand-new school building. After 1694, Magdalen Hall

Opposite:
The inside of
J. C. Buckler's
schoolroom in
the 1850s.

and Magdalen College had had almost nothing to do with each other. The Hall, however, still stood on College land, and one side of its quad contained the School. Then in 1805, Hertford College went bankrupt, and its Catte Street site fell vacant. By 1813 Magdalen College had persuaded Magdalen Hall to take over the Hertford site. That move took time to achieve and the foundation stone at Catte Street was laid in May 1820. As if to hasten Magdalen Hall on its way, its old buildings were badly damaged by a fire in 1821. In the fire the original schoolroom was destroyed. For a while, the School occupied the ground floor of the mid-seventeenth-century house formerly occupied by principals of Magdalen Hall. This temporary accommodation proved rather longer lasting than might have been anticipated. It was not until November 1843 that the President and Fellows decided to erect a new school and house for the Master on the site of the Greyhound Inn, situated on the corner with Longwall Street. The ulterior motive was clear enough: by moving the School buildings further to the west, the College might expand onto the former site of Magdalen Hall (St Swithun's).[4]

J. C. Buckler (artist and architect long connected with the College) was commissioned to design these buildings, but only a few months later the College changed its mind and advertised an open competition. Designs are known from Thomas Allom and John Macduff Derick (George Gilbert Scott also competed, but his designs are lost). Augustus Pugin submitted designs too, at the behest of his friend John Bloxam, but did not intend them to be entered into the competition.[5] J. C. Buckler did not compete at all, presumably piqued at this ill-disguised rejection. John Derick's plan, which was accepted, included a Master's house, a schoolroom, a large hall, a dormitory for the choristers, and a dormitory for other pupils. It would have created a worthy new home for the School. In preparation for the new buildings, the Greyhound Inn was demolished, as were the other houses along the Gravel Walk and the former Principal's Lodgings of Magdalen Hall, so that the School had to be moved to rooms in Chaplain's Quadrangle in the interim.[6]

Edward Ellerton, Usher 1795–98 and Master 1798–1810. Oil on canvas, c. 1780.

Opposite: J. E. Millard, Master 1846–64, a keen bibliographer, helped rebind and preserve many of the School's more antique texts, which now reside in the School archive.

Overleaf: The buildings originally adjoining Magdalen College prior to 1845, including the famous Greyhound Inn on the far left. These buildings were demolished to make way for the 1851 schoolroom. Watercolour attributed to William Turner of Oxford (1807–62).

Unfortunately, at this moment someone chose to ask some awkward questions about the nature of the School. George Parsons Hester, the town clerk of Oxford, and a former chorister at Magdalen from 1807 to 1814, had long taken an interest in the School's affairs.[7] As news of Derick's plans became known, Hester posed a question: just what kind of institution was Magdalen College School? As he would have known, the Founder's statutes indicated that the Master and Usher were to give free lessons in grammar to all comers. When the School was new, this offer had undoubtedly been taken up by young men studying in the University, and by the sons of local city families. By the 1840s, however, it was usual for pupils who were not choristers to pay for their education. Derick's design, with its second dormitory, suggested to Hester that Magdalen College School was turning into an exclusively private school, in defiance of the statutes. He also suspected – rightly – that the stipends of the Master and Usher had not risen at the same rate as those of the Fellows.[8] In March 1845, therefore, Hester submitted a petition to the Court of Chancery, objecting to the College's actions, and claiming, amongst other things, that 'the suppression of the said Grammar School at Oxford is a public evil to the said City and also the whole realm'.[9]

Hester's assertion that Waynflete's statutes were being flouted was not unreasonable, but on the other hand the educational circumstances of the 1840s were very different from those of the 1480s: Magdalen was not the only school which now allowed, if not encouraged, the presence of fee-paying pupils.[10] Furthermore, the College could argue that, since this matter related to its statutes, only the Bishop of Winchester as Visitor could determine it. Indeed, in June 1847, the Court of Chancery itself agreed that it had no right to decide the case, and referred it to the Visitor. However, the Court did refuse to award costs against Hester, noting that the interpretation

Opposite: The old Grammar Hall after the demolition of Waynflete's original schoolroom. To the left are the President's Lodgings of Magdalen Hall. Hand-coloured etching with engraving, by F. C. Lewis after F. Mackenzie, published in the *Oxford Almanack* for 1842.

Charles Richard Sumner, Bishop of Winchester, involved with the School as Visitor in 1849. Portrait by Sir Martin Archer Shee, 1832.

Architectural sketch by Augustus Pugin in 1843. The drawing depicts Pugin's vision of the exterior of the renovated schoolroom. From a set of fifteen drawings in graphite, pen and ink, 1840–48, commissioned by the College.

No 2.

of the statutes was doubtful, and that the College clearly intended to improve the situation of the School.[11] The wheels of justice moved slowly. Two years passed, during which Hester indulged in such tail-tweaking activities as threatening to turn up at the School with his son to demand a free education for him, and, on being rebuffed, publicly urging the Visitor to intervene. Finally, in March 1849, the Bishop of Winchester, Charles Sumner, gave his decision. Hester, he considered, had no right to demand a free education for his son at the School, and the College's actions had been correct.[12]

At last the College could proceed to rebuild the School, but this time it showed more caution. It was now agreed that the new school building should 'be exactly of the same dimensions as the former one', and that a house be acquired to accommodate the Master, choristers, and 'other boarders'. Oxford would never see Derick's grand vision; instead it would get a new school hall, built to exactly the same dimensions as the old. Not even George Hester could argue against this. Derick was not given a chance to essay a new design. Instead, five years after being snubbed, J. C. Buckler was asked to design the new building. Buckler was magnanimous: within three weeks he had produced a fine new design in the perpendicular style, and was even happy to accept advice from President Martin Routh (President 1791–1854) on the proportions of its windows. The venerable Routh himself made the short journey to the former site of the Greyhound Inn to lay a foundation stone on 19 September 1849, his ninety-fourth birthday.[13] The new building was formally opened on 1 May 1851 with a celebratory concert. The project had undoubtedly been assisted by the benefaction of Routh's sister, Sophia Sheppard, which met a significant proportion of building costs. The College also created new scholarships for non-singing pupils, and Nos 57 and 58 High Street eventually became a boarding house and a home for the Master. The School was entering a new age.[14]

Opposite: A further Pugin sketch showing his vision for the interior of a new schoolroom.

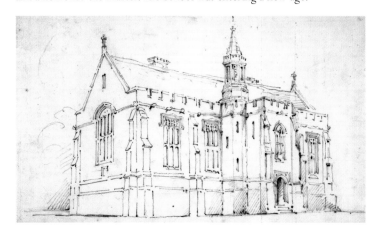

J. C. Buckler's 1849 sketch for the new schoolroom. From the original at Magdalen College.

LOOSENING THE UMBILICAL CORD: 1854–1928

IN THE LATTER part of the nineteenth century, the College continued to be responsible for its three schools: the appointment of the three Headmasters remained nominally in the gift of the President while the schools' accounts were audited by the Bursary.[1] But from 1875 at the latest the general management of the schools was entrusted to a new Schools Committee of the Governing Body, which consisted of the President, Vice-President, Dean of Divinity and Bursar. The surviving minute book reveals that the committee took its duty of care seriously, and supervised the activities of the three schools far more carefully than had been the case hitherto. The schools were subjected to annual visitations – first by private individuals appointed by the College, then by representatives of the Oxford Local Examination Delegacy, and finally by central government inspectors belonging to the Board of Education. Their buildings were kept in a decent state of repair, and the Headmasters and assistant masters were paid reasonable salaries.[2] At the same time, it is evident that Magdalen found the responsibility increasingly irksome. Under the 1870 Education Act, elementary schooling was made compulsory for all boys and girls under the age of thirteen, and its organisation was initially entrusted to the care of local school boards. The three Magdalen schools formed part of a second tier of educational institutions, defined under the 1902 Education Act, which provided advanced tuition for the small proportion of teenagers who did not immediately enter the workforce. Although many if not most of these secondary schools were historically independent of central or local authority control, retention of their status required large injections of cash to bring them up to the state's required standard. Magdalen was initially quite generous to two of its three schools, but by the turn of the twentieth century the College was wary of investing any further for fear of having to commit an ever larger proportion of its income to the maintenance and improvement of their facilities. In consequence, Magdalen looked more and more to local education authorities – the bodies given responsibility for elementary and

Opposite: May Day celebrations on Magdalen Tower. Sydney Prior Hall, wood engraving with tone-plate, 1885.

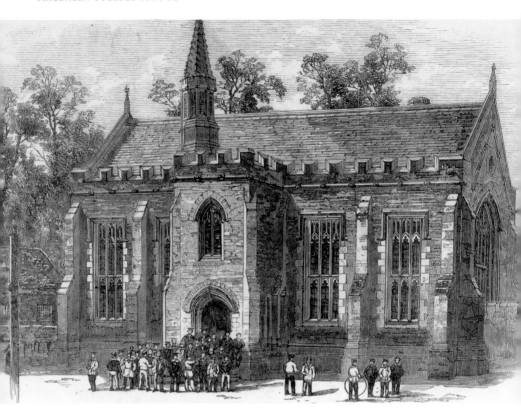

The front of
Magdalen College
School in 1858.
Anonymous,
wood engraving,
published in *News
of the World,* 1858.

secondary education at county level under the 1902 Act – for relief from
this burden. The College salved its conscience by pointing to the restrictions
on school expenditure laid down in its current statutes. According to those
of 1880, no more than £800 a year was to be spent on the Oxford school,
and no more than £500 on the other two combined, sums which were raised
in 1926 to £1,500 and £800 respectively. The College was also aware that,
under the 1880 statutes, it was no longer obliged to maintain the Wainfleet
and Brackley schools, if the running costs got too high.[3]

By the end of the period it is clear that Magdalen would ideally have
liked to have severed even its link with the one school it was enjoined by
statute to maintain. Lying within the curtilage of Magdalen's own site, and
educating its sixteen choristers, the Oxford school was the one with the
closest links to the College, in this period as in the past. It was also the
largest and most expensive to run. Although never a huge school, there
were usually (apart from occasional dips) some eighty to a hundred boys
between the ages of nine and nineteen on the roll. As at Brackley, the
majority were often boarders: sixty-three out of ninety-one in 1865, fifty

out of eighty-one in 1904. But at Oxford the boarding house was of a slightly older vintage, for it had been set up by the College in 1849 in order that the choristers might be properly supervised. It was difficult, even for those who came from Oxford, to live at home and perform their duties in the Choir. Originally the choristers seem to have lived within the College curtilage, but prior to the establishment of the boarding house they had been boarded out in Holywell Street or Longwall.[4] From at least 1883 to the outbreak of war, and possibly beyond, day fees were 18 guineas a year, while boys' parents also paid a supplement of 3 to 4 guineas to support a games fund from the 1880s. Boarders' parents (other than those of College choristers), on the other hand, paid £48 a year for their sons' accommodation in the 1900s, on top of tuition and sports fees. This sum must have risen considerably by the 1920s.[5]

Inevitably, given these costs, most boys came from reasonably prosperous backgrounds. In no sense was it a free school, although the College did cover choristers' board and lodging, and paid initially all, and from 1903 half, their tuition fees.[6] Magdalen College School, Oxford, was therefore seen as an establishment for the sons of professional men, and not those of tradesmen, who were sent to the rival Oxford High School (established 1881) where fees were lower. This perception affected its ability to attract more day boys. There were few potential recruits in the new poorer part of Oxford that was developing to the east of Magdalen Bridge, while boys in fashionable North Oxford were not sent in large numbers because of the distance, and the propinquity to them of a new rival, St Edward's (founded 1863).[7]

In 1877 the annual salary of the Master was set at £250, while the Usher was to receive the same as the Headmasters of Wainfleet and Brackley, £150. By 1912 the sums had risen to £350 and £200 respectively, and there must have been further increases in the 1920s. On top of this the Master and Usher enjoyed shares of the capitation fees, which probably increased their income by another £200 and £100 in pre-war years. The Master, moreover, enjoyed a rent-free house. With the prospect of making further money from the boarding establishment, the headship was an enticing position; when H. C. Ogle (Master 1876–86) retired in 1886, a hundred men applied to take his place.[8] Besides the Master and the Usher, the School in fact supported five assistant masters, one of whom was also the School Chaplain. These were paid, albeit with some difficulty, out of the School's fee income. Before the war they enjoyed annual salaries of £150 to £170, which, although not large, were apparently sufficient to ensure that the staff turnover remained small.[9] In contrast to Brackley, the assistant masters seem always to have been specialist teachers, even if they sometimes had to double up, for appointments recorded in the Schools Committee minute book are certainly subject-specific. In 1890, for instance, separate masters

Christmas celebrations in the College Hall. Joseph Nash, gouache, 1858. The College and its Choir played an important role in establishing Victorian traditions of celebrating Christmas.

were appointed for modern languages, mathematics, mathematics and science, and drawing, the last of whom, B. H. Price (who served part-time), had been an assistant at the Ruskin School of Drawing and Fine Art for twenty years.[10]

Before the final quarter of the nineteenth century there is some suggestion that the School provided only limited instruction in the modern subjects of history, geography and English literature, especially in the upper forms, although science had certainly been part of the curriculum from the mid-1860s.[11] Subsequent Masters did their best to rectify this deficiency, particularly C. E. Brownrigg (Master 1900–30). On taking up office, according to a report he drew up for the College in 1912, he had allowed boys to take German rather than Greek when they began a third language, and introduced

special hours for extra mathematics, as well as making science compulsory for the elementary forms.[12] The report also asserted that from the moment W. E. Sherwood (Master 1888–1900) took over the School, the quality of the teaching had been high. According to Brownrigg, during the twelve years of Sherwood's headship, boys at the School had gained 101 senior certificates, and won twenty-three Oxbridge scholarships and exhibitions. In the following twelve years, under his own control, it had won a further 118, and twenty-six, respectively.[13] As a result, reflecting on these results Brownrigg felt justifiably proud of the School's achievements given its small size:

> In recent years since the revival under Mr. Sherwood – though the
> competition between schools has become more intense and the levelling up

Boys playing with hockey sticks on the old playground. The Master, H. C. Ogle, can be seen standing on the far right.

or down of education has added greatly to the field of competitors – the records are far from discreditable. In entertaining them it must be borne in mind that at least 30% of our small numbers are under the ordinary public school age and that a good many boys come to us with very little 'literary' education.[14]

Much of this achievement must be put down to the efforts of Sherwood and Brownrigg themselves, but part must also be attributed to the College, which throughout the second half of the nineteenth century showed willingness to invest in the School's future, and so laid the foundations of later success. From 1851 the School was housed in the new purpose-built school on the College site, with playground and Fives court. Improvements in the following years were largely paid for independently of the College, for the redbrick chapel which was built close to the school building in 1856/7 was primarily funded by the Old Boys.[15] But in the mid-1890s the College agreed to make a second significant financial contribution to development when it decided to build School House, doubtless a reflection of President Herbert Warren's real enthusiasm for the School.[16] Hitherto, the School's boarding house and Master's residence had been a house on the corner of the High Street and Longwall. Its facilities had been greatly

Opposite:
H. C. Ogle, oil on canvas, c. 1880.

extended by Millard, who had added a dining room and kitchen, and had bought the house next door. He had also constructed a school laboratory in the complex. By the 1890s, however, the boarding house was insufficient for Sherwood's ambitions, and in 1893/4 a new building was erected on Cowley Place on the other side of the Plain (today the School's administrative building), which could accommodate fifty boarders.[17] In 1893, too, the College further helped improve the facilities of the School by arranging with Christ Church to lease its present cricket field on the island in the middle of the Cherwell, although much levelling needed to be done, and it was another ten years before it was fully serviceable – before this the boys had had to travel some distance to play football and cricket.[18] Indeed, Magdalen was even quite happy for the School to use its own facilities. From 1887, if not before, the School's science master taught boys in the Daubeny Laboratory, subject to the consent of Edward Chapman (lecturer then tutor in natural science), because although the boys had a good chemistry laboratory they had nowhere for physics. Two years later this arrangement was cemented with the appointment of J. J. Manley, the Daubeny Curator, as an assistant master. The College allowed him to teach in the School, and to give senior boys advanced tuition in the Daubeny Laboratory.[19] The College also did its best to attract the intellectually gifted to the School. In 1901, it agreed to offer eight full-fee exhibitions, two per year, which would be awarded on the strength of an examination, open to outsiders, in Latin, Greek and mathematics.[20]

The College Governing Body's generosity, however, showed the first signs of wearing thin in 1904. In that year Brownrigg sought support to add two extra classrooms on the Longwall site. At this date the School ran seven forms, or classes. The two upper forms occupied the first floor of the school building, and the three middle forms used the ground floor, the room being trisected by a curtain, while two lower forms were taught in the library of School House. Specialist groups were taken in the boarding house coat lobby. Brownrigg understandably thought this unsatisfactory, and wanted to improve facilities. The Schools Committee was supportive, and recommended that the new classrooms be built on the Longwall rather than the School House site, which was the cheaper option even if it meant using part of the playground. The committee did suggest, however, that Fellows should think long and hard about whether they wanted a growing school on their very doorstep, and whether the College might want the site for its own purposes. The Fellows did consider carefully, and permitted the School to erect two classrooms on its playground, as long as they were only temporary buildings.[21]

Within eight years it is clear that relations between School and College had cooled considerably. The primary bone of contention was funding. The College had done its sums, and discovered that it was spending far more on

Opposite: Master W. E. Sherwood. Thomas Sheard, oil on canvas, c. 1894–1900. Sherwood raised the School's standards at a time when the College was considering cutting the institution adrift.

MCS choristers singing on May morning. Behind them sit a number of College worthies, including John Bloxam, Sir John Stainer and College President Herbert Warren. William Holman Hunt, oil on canvas, c. 1888.

the School than the £800 permitted under the statutes. Thanks to the recent increase in the stipends of the Master and Usher, the new cost of the eight exhibitions, and the cost of amortisation of the £12,940 the College had spent on improving the School in the recent past (£430 a year), Magdalen College School was now costing the College between £1,400 and £1,500 a year.[22] The financial burden, however, was not the only consideration. Two years before, an incident at the School had caused the College serious embarrassment. The College naturally left day-to-day administration of the School to the Master, but it had to interfere occasionally, as when it received a complaint about heavy-handed use of corporal punishment in 1910. In the summer of that year it had become involved in the case of a local doctor's son who had been beaten by the senior prefect for assaulting another prefect. It is not clear if the doctor objected to the punishment as such, but he certainly did object to the instrument with which it had been administered. The College accepted that the (unspecified) instrument should not have been used, but upheld the right of the prefect to punish. The doctor then issued a summons against the senior prefect, one Newton, for assault. He was tried by magistrates in the Oxford Police Court, found guilty and fined 20. Not surprisingly, the local newspapers had a field day. More ominously, the professional community of the city was horrified by the goings-on, and when the School reconvened after the summer, no new

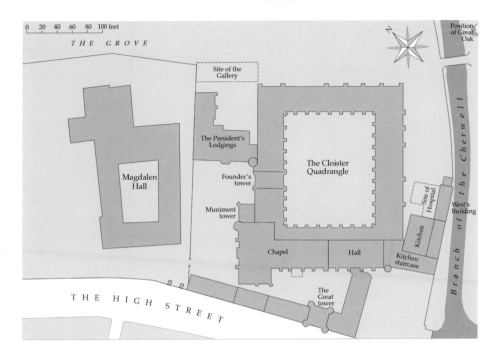

0 20 40 60 80 100 feet

THE GROVE

Site of the Gallery

The President's Lodgings

The Cloister Quadrangle

Magdalen Hall

Founder's tower

Muniment tower

Chapel

Hall

Kitchen staircase

The Great tower

THE HIGH STREET

Position of Great Oak

Branch of the Cherwell

West's Building

Site of Hospital

Kitchen

N

day boys appeared, and numbers fell to seventy. They had shown no signs of recovering two years later.[23]

In June 1912 the Schools Committee took a long hard look at the value of maintaining the College's commitment to its Oxford school. Its initial verdict on the School was damning. On 18 June 1912 'it invited the College to consider whether it is desirable to alter the statute, so as to make it optional for the College to maintain the grammar school at Oxford'.[24] Brownrigg was then asked to provide a written comment on the financial state of the School. Aware that there were some in the College calling for it to be closed, and replaced by a simple choir school, he put up a strong defence. In particular, he pointed out that the annual charge on the buildings sinking fund was really only £140, when the rent that the College received from the vacated boarding house site on the High Street was taken into account. He could not deny, however, that numbers were not as strong as they might be, and that educational opinion had turned in favour of larger schools.[25] The committee now took a softer line. In a report to the College Governing Body, it accepted most of the Master's points, but still insisted that the School was costing the College £1,500 a year. While the charge of amortising the building debt was less than had been supposed, a further £200 had to be added to the bill in the form of the hidden subsidy that the Master received in being allowed to run School House rent free.[26] It was

Map of Magdalen College in 1898. Note the location of Magdalen Hall, Grove and High Street. Drawn by Paul Simmons, adapted from an engraving by H. Hurst, 1898.

In 1926, the efficiency of the Combined Cadet Force was recognised by the War Office, and Brownrigg, who had founded the CCF in the First World War, chose this moment to hand over the command to Major C. H. B. Shepherd MC, seen here inspecting the Force with the Vice Chancellor, F. W. Pember.

also pointed out that at its current size the School did not cover the cost of its teaching; tuition fees did not support the salary of the five assistant masters without the Master and Usher taking a cut in their *per capita* entitlement.[27] None the less, the committee did not suggest that links with the School should be severed immediately. Rather, the College should invite the Board of Education to inspect the School, and take a decision following its report. At this stage its conclusion was simply admonitory: 'They simply desire to remind the College that if the school is to be maintained upon its present scale, it can only be at a cost not contemplated by the existing statutes and bye-laws.'[28]

The outbreak of the First World War seems to have prevented either a permanent decision being taken or any widening of the rift. Magdalen, like every other Oxford and Cambridge college, was devastated and traumatised

Opposite: Charles Edward Brownrigg, Master, who led the School through the First World War. Known informally as 'The Brigger'. Arthur Hayward (?), oil on canvas, c. 1900.

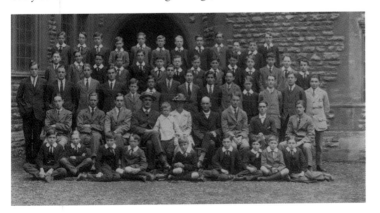

A school photograph from 1919, with Brownrigg, his wife and son front centre. Brownrigg kept in contact with many school leavers, particularly those who were called up to serve in the First World War. Of the MCS alumni who served in the First World War, 20 per cent lost their lives.

by the First World War. Overall some 930 members of the College bore arms in the conflict, and 187 were killed. Many more, of course, of those who had attended one of the College's schools were also killed. Between them, the College and the School nourished three Victoria Crosses, most famously the doctor Noel Chavasse, Old Boy of the School. Chavasse received the honour twice, the second posthumously after dying of wounds in 1917.

The College returned to the issue of its relationship with the School in the years following the conclusion of the peace. It no longer thought of closing the School – there had been enough loss and destruction on the Western Front – but it did look for help in paying the costs. The obvious partner was the local educational authority. There had been discussions with Oxfordshire county council about admitting scholarship boys to the School as early as 1904, and the possibility had been agreed in principle. But there negotiations had stalled, presumably because the county council preferred to buy places in the more central Oxford High School for Boys.[29] Unlike Brackley, the Oxford school had not become grant-maintained in the years before 1914. In 1919, however, the College decided that it would like to bring its largest school within the ambit of the state educational system, and the Central Board of Education was approached to see if any improvements would have to be undertaken, and what arrangements needed to be made for the choristers. The following year the Board accepted the College's request and undertook an inspection. Apart from the need to raise staff salaries in line with the 1920 Burnham pay scale for state teachers, all was found to be in order, though the College was told to create a physics laboratory so that the School would no longer have to use the Daubeny Laboratory. A site was duly found behind 71 High Street, and uninvested capital in the school pension fund was used to equip it. The College also erected a former army hut in the playground as an extra classroom.[30] Thereafter the School, like Brackley, was in receipt of public funds, but never to the same degree.[31]

As Warren (President 1885–1928) prepared to retire there is no evidence that the College was contemplating severing this historic link. It had, however, decided to remove the School from the College site. The College needed more space to accommodate undergraduates, and the School occupied a prime space within the curtilage. If the College was ever to extend to St Swithun's (eventually built in early 1880s) and build a new quadrangle, the School would inevitably have to be relocated. The idea of creating the future Longwall quadrangle had first been mooted towards the end of 1926, and by the spring of 1928 it was College policy. The School was informed that it would have to move to College land on the corner of Iffley Road and Cowley Place on the opposite side of the street to the boarding house.[32]

Opposite: Noel Chavasse, one of only three men to be awarded the Victoria Cross twice. The first was awarded for his bravery treating the wounded during the battle of Guillemont during the 1916 Somme offensive, and the second awarded posthumously in 1917 after Chavasse was fatally wounded while helping casualties on the battlefield in Wieltje, Belgium.

PERIOD OF UNCERTAINTY: 1928-68

IN THE FIRST thirty years of the twentieth century, the Magdalen schools had become increasingly expensive to run. As local educational authorities (LEAs) set up their own grammar schools with good facilities, it became difficult to provide a competitive education to the standards demanded by the Board of Education without a large financial investment. This the College had been reluctant to supply and, further to earlier attempts to divest Magdalen of responsibility for the Wainfleet and Brackley schools, Wainfleet was closed in 1933, and Brackley was handed over to the Northamptonshire County Council in 1949, although the College continued to own the buildings and grounds and was represented on the school's governing body.

Magdalen College School, Oxford (MCS) had lived cheek by jowl with the College from its very foundation, and continued to educate its boy choristers. A surgical separation of these entities was always going to be more problematic than in the other two cases, since here 'gown' interests encountered exceptionally strong 'town' loyalties on their very doorstep. These were difficult to brush aside, and often represented by extremely articulate local Old Boy grandees, like Basil Blackwell, bookseller extraordinary, and Dr John Johnson, printer to the University. As academic salaries went into relative decline, moreover, and Fellows found boarding fees for their sons prohibitively expensive, the School came to serve some members of the College Governing Body in a very practical way by educating their offspring after the Second World War. At least one of those who benefited in this manner, a man of the left, thought the College's neglect of the School scandalous.[1]

Real tension developed between the College and its Oxford school at the very end of Warren's regime, when the Fellowship had decided to appropriate the school site, and construct a new Longwall quadrangle on the old playground. Initially there had been no suggestion that the School would suffer as a result, for the architect, Sir Giles Gilbert Scott, was asked to draw up plans for new buildings to rehouse the School across Magdalen

Opposite: The old library in 1958. Part of a series of photographs taken at the School during that year.

Basil Blackwell, a lifelong friend and ally of the School, always worked to support it, in this case as a rowing coach, 1917.

Bridge at the beginning of the Iffley Road near the existing boarding house. Not surprisingly, the School was enthusiastic about the move, which promised it re-establishment in splendid new facilities.[2] In the course of a conversation with the Master of the School, however, the College Estates Bursar Revd C. R. Carter (Bursar 1910–30) let drop, apparently with relish, the bombshell that the College's responsibility to the School had been materially altered by the 1926 statutes, which allowed the College to terminate its commitment. Even though the Master was on the Foundation he had heard nothing of this, and failure to communicate the news had certainly not been a matter of mere oversight. It was clear that Bursar Carter was by no means committed to a permanent future for the School. He told the Master that the Scott project was likely to cost £40,000; this was far too much for the College to contemplate when, having finally cleared its old debts, Magdalen was about to borrow deeply once again for its own new buildings.

What was not expressed at that time but soon became clear to all was that the College had other reasons to hesitate. The city was believed to be planning two new and well-equipped boys' schools, which might make it impossible to fill the free places required by the Whitehall Board of Education grant. At that time there were only seventy-seven day boys out of a total of 170. Of these, sixteen had places paid for by the city, and twenty by the Board of Education. The School was threatened with the loss of half its local intake. Only one of the ninety-three boarders was an Oxford boy,

Pupils of the twenty-first century outside the so-called Temporary Buildings, opened 1929, intended by the College not to outlast the twentieth.

Opposite: Cosmo Gordon Lang, Archbishop of York and former Dean of Divinity, whom the School asked to represent it during the crisis of 1928–29. Philip Alexius de László, oil on canvas, c. 1900.

and the Bursar was adamant that the College bore no financial responsibility at all for the education of boys from elsewhere.

Basil Blackwell, Secretary of the Old Magdalen College School Club ('Old Waynfletes'), and a favourite former pupil of the Master, Brownrigg, moved rapidly into action. He formed a 'Safeguarding Committee', and successfully requested from President Warren an interview with the College's Schools Committee for a delegation representing the School. The impressive body of delegates comprised the Headmasters of Shrewsbury School, St Edward's School in Oxford, and Ipswich School; the chief cashier of the Bank of England; Professor John Crofts of the University of Bristol; and Blackwell himself – all Old Boys. Most spoke in measured terms as they took turns to express their views, but Crofts shook the committee with a vehement and impassioned diatribe. He was rewarded for his pains by a *sotto voce* remark from one of the younger Fellows present to the effect that 'the College gets absolutely nothing for its fifteen hundred a year'. Crofts suggested that the insidious change in the statutes had been underhand, and felt that the faces of his interlocutors betrayed that some of them agreed. He was soon after to write privately to President Warren pleading against the snatching away of this educational ladder for poor men:

> What the College really proposes is to close the door to men like me . . . in order to improve the condition of men who are already so fortunate as to be your undergraduates. Our opportunity is to be sacrificed to enhance their privilege.

It was to no avail, and the School was forced to make do with much cheaper, and manifestly temporary, buildings. These, designed by Boulton and Paul, were erected on the Iffley Road site, and were just about adequate for so small an institution, but their provisional nature set alarm bells ringing. A sop was offered to the Old Boys as the President informed them in writing that the Schools Committee had been instructed 'to consider what steps, if any, could be taken to safeguard the interests of the School'. However, as Warren readily admitted, this was 'rather vague'. When the School opened its doors on the new site in September 1928, the College was clearly doubtful about its future, a fact that was bound to affect the confidence of the parents, the city educational authority and the Board of Education.

The Old Boys, led by Blackwell, sought to interest both the Archbishop of York, Cosmo Gordon Lang – a former Dean of Divinity – and the Bishop of Winchester, as Visitor, but after contact with Warren the two clerics ended up rather sympathising with the College's predicament. The Safeguarding Committee tried hard to inject elements of permanence into the new arrangements with a view to publicly committing the College to the School's future. They did succeed in having a novel Old Boys' Scholarship Fund accepted, but failed in their more substantive plea for a permanent chapel on the new site, part-funded by them. Instead the College paid for another temporary structure by Boulton and Paul at a cost of only £3,000. This opened in 1929.

The Old Boys were, perhaps naively, convinced that they had the sympathy of the retiring President and of Vice-President Edwin Craig, but the latter could not stand out too visibly against radical younger Fellows like Thomas Weldon if his hopes of succeeding the retiring Warren were to come to anything (despite his efforts Craig wasn't elected). One Fellow, J. M. Thompson, told the Old Boys that they would have to await the retirement of Bursar Carter, then imminent, for any significant change of heart on the part of the College.[3]

In the event the School struggled on through the 1930s, although it was hard hit by the recession in terms of attracting boarders – there were still ten places vacant in 1937/8 – and was producing financial deficits from 1932 onwards. Importantly, however, total numbers on the roll remained more or less steady at about 170 until the Second World War. It was inspected by the Board of Education in March 1932, and on the whole received a very good report.[4]

At the prize-giving on 22 June 1935, the Master of the School appealed to the College once more to put up permanent buildings. This provoked

Interior, by Peter Greenham, pen and ink with wash. c. 1939–45. Probably depicts the shed-like studio where Greenham worked during the Second World War, when employed as an art master at MCS.

little heart searching in the College Governing Body, which was unfortunately just then embarking on an effort to reduce budgetary deficits. In Michaelmas Term 1936, with a view to 'rationalisation of the resources of the College, so that it may make the greatest possible contribution to learning & education', the Fellowship's Sub-Committee on Economy produced a report, dealing among other things with the financing of the two remaining Magdalen College schools. The Schools Committee was asked to find ways of reducing the cost to the College of their upkeep and, together with the Chapel Committee, to consider 'separating the Choir School from Magdalen College School, Oxford, and incorporating it with the New College Choir School'. That absolute economy was not the keynote of this discussion is evident from the same sub-committee's request that another committee be appointed 'to consider what *extensions* of the College's expenditure on higher education and research are desirable'.[5]

Following this up in the summer of 1937 the Schools Committee presented a majority report recommending discontinuance of Magdalen College School. Although in the event the College Governing Body did not consent to act upon the proposal in Michaelmas Term, rumblings of it reached the Old Boys in August. Uncertainty was compounded by a new belief that the LEA was planning to rebuild the City of Oxford Boys' School, which once more raised the threat of powerful competition.[6] The Old Boys were adamant that permanent new buildings must be provided to secure the future of the School, and in January 1938 they appointed a deputation to meet the College Schools Committee. A meeting took place on 17 January, when the College made clear that it could not help financially. Already under the obligation of a very heavy burden of unavoidable academic taxation, such a commitment would not only have required a two-thirds majority decision on the College Governing Body to change the statute limiting its liability to the School to £1,500 p.a., but also the consent of the University, which had a stake in the College's revenue. Fruitless discussions then took place involving the city education authority and other bodies.

Nothing further of substance had occurred when at the School prize-giving in June 1938 Dr John Johnson, printer to the University – Old Boy of the School, senior demy of the College 1909–12, and father of a boy then on the roll – distributed the prizes, and gave a most eloquent address in which he appealed for £20,000 to provide new, permanent brick buildings, and offered to donate £1,000 himself.[7] Soon, following an appeal from the Old MCS Club, £8,000 had been pledged; faced with such enthusiastic generosity the College's Schools Committee had a change of heart, and recommended that MCS be established on a more permanent basis. Colin Hardie, Tutorial Fellow in Classics, wrote to the Master, R. Kennard Davis (Master 1930–44) later in the year saying that Johnson's appeal, which had

Opposite:
R. Kennard Davis, who published a number of poems while Master. Oil on panel, c. 1950.

An ice floe forms
a makeshift raft, to
entertain boarders
in 1940.

been circulated to the whole of the College Governing Body, had been so effective 'that there is no longer (if there ever was) any intention at all to close the School out of hand'. Meanwhile, Johnson had opened a line of communication to the apparently sympathetic W. J. M. Mackenzie, Tutorial Fellow in Politics, and was able to argue his case very effectively and in detail, with some hope that it might reach those who mattered.

An architect's plans were obtained, and Carter's successor as Estates Bursar, Arnold Forster, who had the unfortunate knack of provoking his colleagues at every turn, entered the lists alongside the President, offering fatally warm support. Forster hoped to use the large Mackinnon bequest, which had only recently fallen in, to make the scheme possible.[8] But this annoyed the increasingly powerful Tutorial Board who wanted the new funds to be used for scholarships, including some for graduate students. In November the College Governing Body considered a scheme which would be part financed by a College loan of £10,000, repayable with 3 per cent annual interest out of the statutory annual grant to the School; this in turn would be increased from £1,500 to £1,800. The Bursar argued that the scheme was both financially sound and legal. However on 16 November the Bursarial Committee, to which the scheme had been referred by a majority in favour on Governing Body, refused to recommend it to the College. A formidable grouping of Bruce McFarlane (Fellow and Tutor in Modern History), John Morris (Fellow and Tutor in Law), and Redvers Opie (Tutor in Economics and Home Bursar), realising they were a minority on committee, had met in caucus beforehand to unpick the Bursar's sums and legal assurances. They did this to such effect that at the meeting all the other members turned on the unpopular Forster. At a meeting of Governing Body on 30 November 1938 the proposal to increase the annual MCS grant to £1,800 was indeed passed twenty-one to thirteen, but failed in reality as the two-thirds majority required to seek statutory change had not been attained.

In a private letter revealing the progress of this initiative and its failure, Bruce McFarlane wrote of MCS that:

The left-wing wished to close it
(a) because it was going down hill anyway
(b) because we don't value the Christian & classical education it offers & w[oul]d prefer the city to build a new state secondary school
(c) because we could spend the £1800 p.a. & the proceeds of the £50,000 site better on higher education & secondary education (particularly of that sort) is not our business.[9]

H. M. D. Parker (Vice-President 1938, 1939, 1940) confirmed the history tutor's analysis in his entry in the Vice-President's register for 1938. While disagreeing with the viewpoint of McFarlane and others, he confirmed that 'opposition to the School inside the College rests ... upon the belief that a school is not a proper object upon which to spend College money, which should rather be devoted to subsidizing research'.[10] The College's attitude at this time was enshrined in a new provision made in amending statute XI in 1939–40:

If the College schools in Oxford or at Brackley or either of them shall cease to be maintained and managed by the President and Fellows as aforesaid the President and Fellows shall have power to make such arrangements as they think fit for the winding up of such schools or either of them.[11]

After attempts at compromise, with further correspondence between Johnson and Mackenzie while war was looking ever more likely, the matter was effectively dropped for the time being.[12] Prior to that, however, Johnson

had told a committee meeting of the Old MCS Club in March 1939 that 'only a big bomb c[oul]d now penetrate to the deep dugout of the irresolution of the College'. In an exchange of letters with the President in that same month the doughty fighter remarked, after provocation from expressions used by President Gordon, that he could not 'help feeling that there has been too much talk in the past of wisdom and unwisdom, too little of duties, devotion and ideals'.[13]

The Second World War saw a dramatic and unplanned expansion of MCS, and with it, a transformation of its fortunes. Oxford was regarded as relatively safe from bombing and received many evacuees. In September 1939 numbers at MCS stood at 192, but they rose rapidly thereafter, and classes had to be duplicated from 1941. Moreover, as the increased intake worked its way through, numbers continued to rise by some twenty a year even after the war, until a total of getting on for 400 was reached in 1949, and maintained. Fortunately, Milham Ford Girls' School had moved from the site adjoining MCS to Marston Road in 1938: its hut classrooms, together with several other expedients, provided basic accommodation for the expansion, although facilities remained makeshift and chaotic for quite some time and the quality of the teaching staff was far from ideal.[14] Significantly, too, with the return of safety at the end of the war the number of boarders dwindled considerably, and continued to decline thereafter. Adapting to the changed conditions of the post-war world, the School no longer required choristers to board, if their parents could guarantee their presence at rehearsals, services and concerts.

Sir Henry Tizard, President from 1942, took to heart the need to reach a solution to the problem of MCS, for it was obvious to all that the temporary accommodation could not last or receive official approval for ever. At this time MCS was steadily building up a modest surplus with its new-found prosperity, and the Bursarial Committee wished to adjust the College's contribution so as to keep the School's reserve to the minimum £500 considered necessary for the management of emergency expenses. The Master pleaded for permission to accrue funds that might form the nucleus of a building fund or act as security for a future loan from the College, and Basil Blackwell weighed in with more forceful words than his friend the Master felt able to use, as well as a threat of publicity. The College Meeting of 20 May 1943 compromised by ordering, 'that the Schools Committee be informed that the College does not wish the surplus of the Oxford School Account to exceed £3,000 net, and that they be requested to administer the Schools Fund accordingly'. But this was far from amounting to a commitment to MCS's continuance.[15]

In June 1944, Robert Stanier, who had already been Usher for some years and was the author of a competent history of MCS printed by John

Opposite:
R. S. Stanier.
Oil on canvas,
c. 1944. Master
who dominated
the years after the
Second World War
in a similar fashion
to Brownrigg's
domination of
the First.

Above:
Watercolour by
Robert Stanier,
giving a view of
the College from
Magdalen Bridge.
Watercolour,
1950s.

Johnson, and published by Basil Blackwell in 1940 as a contribution to the struggle for survival, was appointed Master. The Schools Committee warned Stanier that his appointment might be terminated at twelve months' notice, given that by the terms of the Education Act of that year the College was compelled to discuss the future of MCS with the city council, and could not commit itself to his future. The precariousness of his position was enhanced when he found he was expected to purchase the boarding house personally as a going concern, although he was soon able to unload this unreasonable

The new Science
Block, erected by
the School in 1951.

Opposite: Sir Basil
Blackwell, by
former pupil and
teacher Brian
Cairns. Acrylics,
c. 2005. The
painting shows
Blackwell after
the award of his
knighthood in 1956.

responsibility. In the event he was to survive at the helm for twenty-three years, and to steer MCS judiciously to relative stability and security. His very public commitment to the Campaign for Nuclear Disarmament, of which he became local chairman, from the late 1950s may have given him some leverage with radical Fellows of the College like A. J. P. Taylor.[16]

At the end of the war President Tizard, only too aware of the implications of the 1944 Education Act, and conscious that the School required large capital expenditure if it was to continue, spent some time quizzing the Master for data and doing his sums before he convinced the College Governing Body, by a small majority, to offer the School to the city on generous terms. This would at least have scotched the pre-war radical aspiration of McFarlane and others to realise the cash value of the site. Following a number of meetings the city, again by a small majority, asked the College to continue MCS as a direct grant school under the new and more generous terms of the 1944 Act. The College agreed, by yet another small majority, and in the event MCS operated as a direct grant school until the 1970s. The Vice-President noted that, 'This decision commits us to rebuild the School when priority can be given, but I am quite sure that College policy will change many times before that happens'.[17] This move led to 25 per cent of places being offered free to pupils, fully paid for by the city and neighbouring LEAs, whose representatives sat on the Schools Committee. The LEAs also took up a number of boarding places. In principle, no really able local boy would henceforth be debarred from entering the School because of parental inability to pay the fees.

Crucially, in the post-war years the College's Senior Bursar C. A. Cooke was not one of those who wished to dispose of the School, and he was inclined to be helpful providing it did not cost the College too much.[18] Direct grant schools were now permitted by the Ministry of Education to borrow for building purposes, and to fix fees at a level permitting repayment of the loans over a number of years. A new concrete school building was put up in 1951, and the playground was resurfaced.[19] In December 1954, with the security afforded by the government's new financial arrangements, the College agreed – once the worst of the post-war restrictions on building licences and materials had been lifted – to lend £30,000 to MCS for construction, to be repaid by annual instalments of £2,000 plus interest.[20] A new uncompromisingly modern classroom block was ready for occupation in early 1957. MCS was also able to obtain grants for a block of chemistry and physics laboratories from the Industrial Fund for the Advancement of Science in Schools, which, with help from the College, had financed their commission and building by 1958.[21] The new buildings put up between 1955 and 1958 were designed by David Booth. The next big scheme was for the construction of a new chapel and hall block, and a rather successful

Opposite top:
A junior classroom in 1958.

Opposite bottom:
The playground in the same year.

College President
T. S. R. Boase, a
great supporter
of the School in
a time when many
of his colleagues
wanted to dispose
of it. Anthony
Devas, oil on
canvas, c. 1953.

appeal for £60,000 was launched. Building of what would from then onwards be called 'Big School' took place between 1964 and 1966, with John Pinckheard as architect. By the end of this period MCS had permanent and decent, if far from luxurious, physical provision for its purposes.[22]

A large part of the School's success in the last two decades of the period must be attributed to President T. S. R. Boase (President 1947–68) who, unlike his two predecessors, was quietly but effectively supportive of the link between College and School, and managed to head off the divorce still favoured by some on the Governing Body, even by men whose own offspring had benefited from education at the School.[23] Boase well deserved the dedication to him of the enlarged 1958 second edition of Robert Stanier's history of MCS. Moreover, under Stanier's shrewd management the School was adept at maximising its support base. At his suggestion a parents' association was set up during the academic year 1956/7, and soon proved a valuable asset. Then a new body, the 'Friends of Magdalen College School', was established in December 1959. This was distinct from the long-established Old Waynfletes, and the recent parents' association, and had been created with a view to fundraising for the new chapel and hall.[24] Attempts were also made to make the parents of the boys feel they had some link with the College. A music master, Christopher Bishop, adroitly transferred the annual carol service from the School chapel to the College chapel, where it became a popular event.

Big School on its
opening in 1966.

Storm clouds still loomed occasionally. In 1956 there was an unexpected threat to the playing fields and boarding house in the shape of the new relief road that the government planned to run through Christ Church Meadow. This was only averted as the result of great local opposition, in which the Master, Robert Stanier, was much to the fore.[25] A much graver threat to the School's existence was soon to unfold in the shape of the ramifications of the ending of the direct grant system by the post-1964 Labour government, and its plans for the 'comprehensivisation' of secondary schools.

Stanier and his wife Maida on their last day at the School. The energetic Maida was the author of a large number of plays performed by the pupils while her husband was Master.

Alan Tammadge, front middle, Master 1967–72, with the Senior Common Room.

TOWARDS THE PRESENT: 1968–2008

IN 1968 MCS was still a direct grant grammar school, receiving funds from the local education authority. In consequence, the College made very little financial commitment to its day-to-day running. The then Labour government's dislike of such schools, and the evidence that the succeeding Tory administration of 1970–74 equally saw little value in their continuation, made it clear that MCS's direct grant status would soon lapse, and that a decision would have to be taken about its future. In June 1972, rather than hand MCS over to the LEA, the College voted by twenty-six to thirteen to allow the School to go fully independent when the time came, so long as this did not involve the College in future heavy expenditure. Six months before, the Governing Body had also made clear that the College would cede rent-free use of land and buildings on its Iffley Road site to the School, but without subsidy, beyond a by then paltry annual sum of £2,300. The School was also to pay back, over a period of fifteen years, £80,000 that it had borrowed previously.[1] As a result, when MCS finally became a private school in 1976, under the 1974–79 Labour government, it was essentially left on its own. It had fine playing fields, but its buildings were for the most part little more than a set of crumbling huts, with the notable exception of Big School, the hall-cum-chapel block which had been erected in 1964–66. This was hardly an adequate dowry for a school competing with nearby Abingdon, Radley and St Edward's for pupils. William Waynflete would certainly not have been amused.

The Fellows, however, were collectively tired of the School even before the onset of financial crisis in the mid-1970s. The majority were happy to be freed of responsibility, and even if the more left-wing of them were forced to agree that the School should not be handed over to the local education authority, they were determined that it should be given no portion of the College endowment. Admittedly, MCS was not wholly abandoned. When an appeal was launched in 1970 for a music school and biology laboratories, the College contributed £25,000 of the £100,000 raised, in instalments.

Opposite: A service for new boys held in Magdalen College's chapel. The chapel remains an important link between the School and the College.

73

Then in 1980 on the eve of the School's 500th anniversary, when a fresh appeal was made for funds to modernise and adapt School House, improve sports facilities, and build new science laboratories, the College allowed MCS the use of 13 acres of land at Sandford-on-Thames for an extra sports field. It also agreed that £15,000 should be given to bring the facility up to scratch. It was estimated that this gesture amounted to the equivalent of the £75,000 in hard cash that the Master of the School, Bill Cook, had asked the College to donate to get the appeal rolling.[2]

Initially, even after 1976, MCS continued to be managed by the College School Committee, but this arrangement came to an end in 1987. In that year MCS became a limited charitable company. The School would still be owned by the College, but it would be run by fourteen governor directors, of whom only four were to be Fellows.[3] Although the first chairman of the new Governing Body, Angus Macintyre, was a College Fellow, and a number of Fellows sent their sons to the School in the following years, thereafter MCS and its activities quickly disappeared from the College administrative radar. Even when Magdalen's finances improved there was no collective enthusiasm among the Fellowship for the diversion of any significant portion of the new wealth towards the School, although a further £25,000 was contributed in three instalments to an appeal for another laboratory in 1989.[4] Above all, the College refused utterly to surrender the freehold of a

Opposite: William Cook, Master, took part in raising funds for the Quincentenary buildings by taking part in a 500-mile sponsored bicycle ride. Oil/acrylic on canvas, by Claire Haigh, 1991.

Staff and pupils in the computer room. *The Lily,* 1984.

Opposite: A page
from *The Lily*
of September
1982 showing
four exceptional
teachers, from left
to right, top to
bottom: Jon Brown,
Duncan Smith,
Stephen Spowart
and Freddie
Barrett.

Logo by Korky
Paul for the
School's 525
celebration which
serendipitously
coincided with a
rise in the School's
fortunes.

prime urban site. In 1995, however, accepting that the School needed security of tenure if it were to attract funding to improve its buildings, it did agree that MCS could hold the Iffley Road site at a peppercorn rent for two hundred years, and that it would not be wound up while it remained viable.[5]

To all intents and purposes the College washed its hands of MCS from 1987. Had it not been for the fact that the College still partly paid for the education of the boy choristers, the historic connection between School and College would have been, effectively, at an end. The College agreed to pay only half the school fees of choristers, which inevitably had an effect on the social background of the Choir. By the turn of the century, they were all local boys, for the School closed the boarding house. There were by then hardly any boarders, and the building needed refurbishing on health and safety grounds. Thanks to the success of the Choir appeal, two thirds of the fees were thereafter remitted.

Thanks to this one remaining link, the Master and his deputy, the Usher, retained an attachment to the Foundation – as members of the SCR, enjoying limited dining rights, and with annual invitations to the Restoration Dinner. The School, moreover, was permitted to hold its annual carol service in the chapel (although its annual commemoration service was held in the University Church).

The first intake at the Junior School, 1993.

In the 1970s and 1980s, this continued association, however weak, was almost entirely to the advantage of the School. Prospective parents were more willing to turn a blind eye to poor facilities, given the School's illustrious bigger brother, and the School had no difficulty in recruiting and retaining dedicated and effective teachers.[6] In the 1990s, however, MCS began to prosper and step out from the College's shadow. Until then it had lived from hand to mouth: in order to attract pupils in sufficient numbers, it had had to keep its fees below those charged by the rival Abingdon School, and had struggled to keep its annual balance sheet in the black.

From the mid-1990s, however, under a new Master, Peter Tinniswood (Master 1991–98), and a dynamic chairman of governors with a good business head, John Leighfield, determined efforts were made to create a school worthy of its historic name.[7]

A junior department was opened, which eventually took boys from seven. Until then younger choristers had been taught on their own. This was a peculiar arrangement, and it is surprising that the College did not transfer them to New College School in 1972, breaking its connection with MCS entirely.

With the assistance of a number of wealthy Old Boys who had the same loyalty to MCS that Basil Blackwell had shown over many decades,

Opposite: Spring in their stride: the end of boarding enabled the creation of the Junior School and with it a full educational provision for the chorister.

79

Master Peter Tinniswood (left) with Head of Biology Tony Hollander.

Opposite: Andrew Halls by the White Bridges.

a very ambitious new appeal was launched to raise £5 million in the course of ten years, with a view to bringing all the buildings up to a high standard. This was highly successful, and the site was transformed, culminating in the opening of the Colin Sanders Building in 1998.[8] Tinniswood moved on to Lancing College in that year, but his successor Andrew Halls (Master 1998–2007) proved very capable, and the building programme continued to advance. A new £2,000,000 sports complex was opened in July 2001. In 2002, a new physics laboratory and ICT centre was established, followed by the Sir Basil Blackwell Library in September 2005. In 2008, the School opened a £5 million building housing a spacious refectory, porter's lodge, learning support facilities, staff common room, and the art and design department. In the space of a decade the School had been almost completely refurbished.

More importantly, assisted by a media-savvy Usher, Richard Cairns, and yet another dedicated chair of governors, Michael Peagram, Halls set about improving academic standards. The independent MCS had always attracted bright pupils, but in an age of government league tables the boys had seemed to perform less well in GCSE and A-level examinations than their sisters at Oxford High School. Halls aimed to place MCS at the top of the academic league. He developed the fledgling Junior School, tightened entry standards, and pushed senior boys hard, sometimes to the regret of the older members of staff, who preferred the more laissez-faire regime of his predecessors. He and the governors also seriously began to discuss admitting female pupils. This had been something aired on and off for twenty years but never taken forward out of deference to the feelings of the independent girls' schools in the city who feared the effect on their clientele. The governors, however, believed that this was a decision that could not long be deferred: many independent boys' schools were taking girls in the sixth form; it made good

economic sense; and female students would bring a new and positive dimension to the School.

Halls was stunningly successful. There was a fitting irony here. At the beginning of the twenty-first century, the School in which Magdalen College had lost interest thirty years before, as a social embarrassment, had become a centre of excellence. More to the point, it had become an academic brand in the public mind. No one, of course, visited MCS to gawp at its new but functional buildings, but in 2005 *The Sunday Times* named MCS independent school of the year. Times have changed emphatically.

Opposite top: MCS Common Room, 2001, including new Usher Richard Cairns (to Andrew Halls's right), and the new Head of the Junior School, John Place, fifth row, far right.

Opposite bottom: The New Building opened by Andrew Halls in 2008, following a successful fundraising campaign.

Leavers' Day 2012. The picture includes the first girl cohort, which, although not admitted until 2010, reflected a decision made in principle by the Master and Governing Body several years earlier.

ENDNOTES

THE GRAMMAR SCHOOL AND THE NEW LEARNING
1480–1688

1. Unless otherwise stated, this section is based on N. Orme, *Education in Early Tudor England: Magdalen College and its School, 1480–1540* (Oxford: Magdalen College, 1998).

2. Orme, *Education in Early Tudor England: Magdalen College and its School* (1998), 40. The Gravel Walk (as the name implies) was a wide gravel footpath between the London road and the buildings on the Magdalen site to the west of the College proper. It appears to have been laid out with trees in the late seventeenth century, as it is first mentioned in a lease of 1681: H. E. Salter (ed.), *A Cartulary of the Hospital of St John the Baptist* (3 vols; OHS, lxvi, lxviii and lxix; Oxford, 1914–17), i, 151. It may, though, date from a century earlier.

3. *Statutes of the colleges of Oxford with royal patents of foundation; injunctions of visitors and catalogues of documents relating to the University, preserved in the Public Record Office: Magdalen College* (Oxford, 1853), 76.

4. Orme, *Education in Early Tudor England: Magdalen College and its School* (1998), 45–47; Stanier, *Magdalen School* (Oxford, 1958), 47.

5. T. A. R. Evans, 'The Number, Origins and Careers of Scholars', in J. I. Catto and R. Evans (eds.), *The History of the University of Oxford, vol. 2: Late Medieval Oxford* (Oxford, 1992), 485–538: 525–26; A. B. Cobban, 'Colleges and Halls 1380–1500', in Catto and Evans (eds.), *The History of the University of Oxford, vol. 2* (1992), 581–634: 613–14; N. Selwyn, 'Education', in A. Crossley (ed.), *A History of the County of Oxford: Volume IV The City of Oxford* (Victoria County History; London, 1979), 442–62: 442.

6. Magdalen College Archives (MCA), CP/8/49, f. 16r; MCA, *Liber Computi* 1483/4, f. 70r; Anon., *Compendium totius Grammatice ex Laurentio Valla, Servio et Perotto*. The title is significant. Servius was a fourth-century AD grammarian, while Perroto, like Valla, was a fifteenth-century Italian humanist. A. B. Emden, *A Biographical Register of the University of Oxford to A.D. 1500* (3 vols; Oxford, 1957–59), i, 30, *sub* Anwykill.

7. Cobban, 'Colleges and Halls 1380–1500' (1992), 613–14.

8. [J. Anwykill], *Vulgaria quedam abs Terentio in Anglicam linguam traducta*, published in the same year as the *Compendium*.

9. MCA, EL/1, fs 54v–55r. The text of the contract is published in J. R. Bloxam, *A Register of the Presidents, Fellows, Demies, Instructors in Grammar and in Music, Chaplains, Clerks, Choristers, and Other Members of St. Mary Magdalen College*

in the University of Oxford, from the Foundation of the College to the Present Time (7 vols; Oxford, 1853–85), ii, 7–9. Anwykyll had a wife and children, and must have resided in the city.

10. Scarbott, Wolsey, and Jackson were Fellows. Scarbott (demy 1484; Fellow 1486) is the only one of the five to have left hard evidence of the content of his teaching while in charge of the School: Orme, *Education in Early Tudor England: Magdalen College and its School* (1998), 34–35. Brinknell became a canon of Lincoln in 1511: Emden, *A Biographical Register of the University* (1957–59), i, 268.

11. Emden, *A Biographical Register of the University* (1957–59), iii, 1754/5. Brinknell was Master of St John's Hospital from 1511 until 1539: *ibid.*, i, 268.

12. There are 107 printings of Stanbridge's works, but only eight of Anwykyll's are known: Orme, *Education in Early Tudor England: Magdalen College and its School* (1998), 57.

13. N. Orme, *Medieval Schools from Roman Britain to Renaissance England* (New Haven and London, 2006), 118–27.

14. Thomas More has been claimed as an alumnus of the College School, if not of the College itself, but there is no formal record of this: Stanier, *Magdalen School* (1958), 58–61.

15. *Institutio compendiaria totius grammaticae*. For the three grammarians, see Emden, *A Biographical Register of the University* (1957–59), i, 190–91; ii, 1147; and iii, 2039–40. Birchynshaw eventually became tutor to Wolsey's illegitimate son.

16. Whittinton's sojourn at Magdalen College School is recorded in A. Wood (ed.) P. Bliss, *Athenæ Oxonienses: An Exact History of All the Writers and Bishops who have had their Education in the University of Oxford* (4 vols, London, 1813–20), i, 55, but Orme, *Education in Early Tudor England: Magdalen College and its School* (1998), 57, is sceptical as there is no contemporary evidence of a connection with the College.

17. A. Wood (ed.) J. Gutch, *The History and Antiquities of the Colleges and Halls in the University of Oxford* (2 vols; Oxford, 1786), 684, 691 and Appendix, 326; S. G. Hamilton, *Hertford College* (London, 1903), 101–05. In other words, it was another way for a Fellow to earn. For the halls, see esp. J. I. Catto, 'The Triumph of the Halls in Fifteenth-Century Oxford', in R. Evans (ed.), *Lordship and Learning: Studies in Memory of Trevor Aston* (Woodbridge, 2004). Magdalen Hall eventually became Hertford College. Stanier, *Magdalen School* (1958), 20–22, treats the Hall as having initially been the School's hostel. Probably the first principal was John Roper (1492–94), who was a Magdalen Fellow 1483–*c*. 1506, and the University's first Lady Margaret Professor of Divinity, 1502–*c*. 1508; in 1506/7 he seems to have lived in College as a commoner: Emden, *A Biographical Register of the University* (1957–59), iii, 1590; G. D. Duncan, 'Public Lectures and Professorial Chairs', in J. McConica (ed.), *The History of the University of Oxford, vol. 3: The Collegiate University* (Oxford, 1986) iii, 335–61: 350; MCA, CP/8/51, n.p.

18. Orme, *Education in Early Tudor England: Magdalen College and its School* (1998), 7.

19. *Thesaurus linguae romanae & Britanniae*, first edn (London, 1565). *Oxford Dictionary of National Biography (ODNB), sub* Robertson and Cooper.

20. Stanier, *Magdalen School* (1958), 72, 84.

21. Demies were usually at least fifteen or sixteen years old when chosen, but a few were considerably younger. It is impossible to know how many demies studied at the School, but the younger ones who came up in their early teens must have done so.

22. Scholasticism continued to dominate higher study in the French universities throughout the early modern period: see L. W. B. Brockliss, *French Higher Education in the Seventeenth and Eighteenth Centuries: A Cultural History* (Oxford, 1987), esp. chs. 4–7. On the growing absorption of the new learning into establishment culture, see esp. A. Grafton and L. Jardine, *From Humanism to the Humanities* (London, 1986).

23. J. K. McConica, 'The Rise of the Undergraduate College', in McConica (ed.), *The History of the University of Oxford, vol. 3: The Collegiate University* (1986), 1–68: 23.

24. *ODNB, sub nom.*; Emden, *A Biographical Register of the University* (1957–59), ii, 827–30.

25. The University as a whole was more reluctant to embrace the new learning than many of its continental sisters: see J. M. Fletcher, 'The Faculty of Arts' in McConica (ed.), *The History of the University of Oxford, vol. 3: The Collegiate University* (1986), 158–99: 157–60. Apart from the foundation of Corpus and Cardinal College, the first real fillip to the study of Greek and Hebrew came with the foundation of the Regius chairs in 1540 which carried a salary of £40 each: G. D. Duncan, 'Public Lectures and Professorial Chairs' in McConica (ed.), *The History of the University of Oxford, vol. 3: The Collegiate University* (1986), 335–61: 344–45.

26. Pointedly, Wolsey chose as his first professor of divinity at Cardinal College not a Magdalen Fellow but a former Master of Magdalen College School, Thomas Brinknell, who had been picked by the king to write against Luther in 1521/2. Claymond appears not to have known Greek: S. Allen, H. M. Allen. H. W. Garrod, B. Flower, E. Alföldi-Rosenbaum (eds.), *Opus epistolarum Des. Erasmi Roterodami* (Oxford, 1906–58), iii, 619.

27. The salary and benefits of the Master and Usher are recorded in the *Libri Computi* each year under *stipendia lectorum*. For a list of Masters and Ushers, Stanier, *Magdalen School* (1958), 233–35. One Usher, John Harley, also took up the post after he had been a Fellow.

28. Bloxam, *A Register* (1853–85), iii, 90: Dr Layton to Cromwell. The letter is summarised in *LPFD Henry VIII*, ix (1535), 117 (12 Sept.). Twenty Fellows had written to Cromwell three days before expressing a desire for a praelectorship

in Greek: The first praelectors in Greek were Michael Drumme and John Armstrong who taught in 1538/9: MCA, *Liber Computi* 1538/9, f. 130v.

29. William Lily learnt Greek in Rhodes on returning from a pilgrimage: Emden, *A Biographical Register of the University* (1957–59), ii, 1147. Edward Wotton (Fellow 1516–c. 1524), who was appointed Greek lecturer at Corpus Christi College in 1521/2, must have learnt the language in Oxford. Clearly he felt ill-equipped, for in 1524/5 he travelled in Italy to study the language before resuming the lectureship: A. B. Emden, *A Biographical Register of the University of Oxford A.D. 1501–1540* (Oxford, 1974), 639. Another Fellow from the early 1520s who appears to have known Greek by the time he left Oxford was Starkey: see [old] *DNB, sub nom.*

30. Stanier, *Magdalen School* (1958), 100, 113–14; Bloxam, *A Register* (1853–85), v, 36–40. Harmar was a puritan and became Oxford's Regius Professor of Greek during the Interregnum: see *ODNB, sub nom.*

31. Stanier, *Magdalen School* (1958), 112, 113 and 123.

32. Bloxam, *A Register* (1853–85), iii, 129–33: several Fellows told the bishop that the School had been run down for ten years, and Humphrey was ordered to have a new Master in place by Christmas.

33. Evidence from the *Libri Computi, sub stipendia lectorum.* Presumably he gave the Greek lecture in College.

THE QUIET YEARS 1688–1854

1. For a fuller account of the School from 1689 to 1854 than is given here, see Stanier, *Magdalen School* (1958), 90–159.

2. Bloxam, *A Register* (1853–85), iii, 260. Full notice: *ibid.*, 259–61.

3. MCA, MC:F21/MS1/1.

4. On the temporary accommodation: Bloxam, *A Register* (1853–85), iii, 265. For the new school: *Acta*, 15 Nov. 1843. These events are described more fully in R. H. Darwall-Smith, 'Thomas Allom and the Building of Magdalen College School', *Magdalen College Record* (2002), 85–97. The Greyhound Inn had been on the site since 1526, when it began life as the Cardinal's Hat: A. Crossley (ed.), *A History of the County of Oxford (VCH)*, iv (London, 1979), 438.

5. MCA, *Acta*, 1 Feb. and 3 May 1844. Pugin's designs are in the archives of Magdalen College School, and Derick's and Allom's in the Magdalen College archives (MC:FA17/2/1AD/1 and MC:FA17/2/2AD/1). See R. White and R. H. Darwall-Smith, *The Architectural Drawings of Magdalen College Oxford: A Catalogue* (Oxford, 2001), 124–28 (Pugin), 129–36 (Derick), and 136 (Allom).

6. On the progress of plans: MCA, *Acta*, 11 Dec. 1844 and 25 Jul. 1845. On relocation of the School, Bloxam, *A Register* (1853–85), iii, 285.

7. Very short notice in Bloxam, *A Register* (1853–85), i, 212.

8. For most of the period the Master received £23 6s 8d, and the Usher £10 p.a. It was only from 1766/7 that the full sum was listed in the *Libri Computi*, *sub impensae praelectorum*. Before this, the Master's stipend was £10 p.a. and the Usher's £5, as it had been since 1480; the difference was recorded *sub imp. solutionum intrinsecarum et extrinsecarum* as a supplement; initially the Master had only received £20 altogether.

9. Hester's original petition: MCA, MCS/O/27.

10. For the emergence of Eton, Winchester, etc as fee-paying schools, see *int. al.*, J. Chandos, *Boys Together: English Public Schools, 1800–64* (Oxford, 1985).

11. The judge's opinion is printed in full in Bloxam, *A Register* (1853–85), iii, 278–85.

12. Hester's broadsheet, and texts of his letters are bound into MCA, MCS/O/26. For the Visitor's reply: Bloxam, *A Register* (1853–85), iii, 285.

13. For new proposals: MCA, *Acta*, 4 May 1849. On Buckler's plans submitted: MCA, *Acta*, 24 May 1849. For Buckler's design: MCA, MC:FA17/3/1AD/16 and MC:FA1/9/4P/1, fs 11–12; cf. White and Darwall-Smith, *The Architectural Drawings of Magdalen College* (2001), 75–78. For Routh's advice: BL MS Add. 27,963, f. 27 (MS 441, f. 36). On the laying of the foundation stone: Bloxam, *A Register* (1853–85), iii, 290 and MCA, MS 881 (v), no. 36 (an order of service).

14. For the opening of a new school hall: Bloxam, *A Register* (1853–85), iii, 290–91. On Mrs Sheppard's money: *Acta*, 7 Nov. 1851. On school scholarships: MCA, *Acta*, 26 Jul. 1849. For the purchase of 57 and 58 High Street: Stanier, *Magdalen School* (1958), 154, and MCA, EMD 11.3.9. By the mid-nineteenth century the choristers no longer lived within the curtilage, but were boarded out in houses on Longwall and Holywell Street: Stanier, *Magdalen School* (1958), 144–45.

LOOSENING THE UMBILICAL CORD 1854–1928

1. This section complements, but does not replace, accounts given in Stanier, *Magdalen School* (1958), E. G. Forrester, *A History of Magdalen College School, Brackley, Northamptonshire, 1548–1949* (Buckingham, 1950), and B. Parry-Jones and D. Wales, *Magdalen College School Wainfleet 1484–1984* (Grimsby, 1984).

2. MCA, SCCM/1/1–3: minutes 1876–1928. The Oxford Local Examinations Delegacy was set up by statute of Convocation in 1857.

3. *Statutes made for Magdalen College, Oxford, by the University of Oxford Commissioners acting in pursuance of the Universities of Oxford and Cambridge Act, 1877* (Oxford, 1882): MS 703/3, sect xii, nos 1, 2 and 8; *Statutes made for Magdalen College, Oxford, by the University of Oxford Commissioners and by the College under the Universities of Oxford and Cambridge Act, 1923* (Oxford, 1926): MS 703/6(e), sect xi, nos 1 and 8.

4. Stanier, *Magdalen School* (1958), 138–39; SCCM/1/2, 104: 13 Dec. 1904.

5. MCA, SCCM/1/3: 20 Jul. 1920; the boarding fee to be raised by £10, but with no indication of the level at which it had stood after wartime inflation.

6. MCA, SCCM/1/1: 7 Feb. 1903.

7. Names and backgrounds of boys entering both the Brackley and Oxford schools are listed in Schools Committee minutes. The possibility of encouraging tradesmen's sons was discussed by the committee in 1897, but it was decided that no one should be admitted who had not satisfied the Master in an examination: MCA, SCCM/1/1: 8 Feb. 1897. The City of Oxford High School for Boys was established in 1881 as a day school: it was maintained by Oxford City Council.

8. *Ibid.*, 23 Sept. 1885 and 11 Nov. 1886; MCA, SSCM/1/2: 27 Nov. 1912, attached 'Report of School Committee on College School at Oxford' (printed), p. 4 (return from capitation fees). Until 1907 the Master had to pay rent to the College for the use of the boarding house.

9. MCA, SCCM/1/2: 27 Nov. 1912, attached Schools Committee 'Report', p. 4.

10. MCA, SCCM/1/1: 13 Feb. and 27 Oct.1890.

11. *Ibid.*, 20 Oct. 1876.

12. MCA, SCCM/1/2: Brownrigg's report (n. p.), attached to the minutes of 30 Oct. 1912.

13. *Ibid.*, Sherwood had attracted some first-class assistant masters, who included A. E. Cowley (later Bodley's librarian), A. W. T. Perowne (later Bishop of Worcester), P. S. Allen (later Master of Corpus Christi Cambridge) and A. L. Dixon (Waynflete Professor of Mathematics and Fellow from 1922).

14. *Ibid.*

15. Stanier, *Magdalen School* (1958), 157–58.

16. At the prize-giving of 1887, the President had explicitly compared the opportunities for young men at Magdalen College School to those he himself had enjoyed at Clifton: *ibid.*, 181.

17. *Ibid.*, 157–58 and 181–82.

18. See MCA, SSCM/1/2: Brownrigg's report (n.p.), attached to the minutes of 30 Oct. 1912.

19. MCA, SCCM/1/1: 15 Jun. 1887 and 30 Jan. 1889; MCA, SCCM/1/2: Brownrigg's report, attached to the minutes of 30 Oct. 1912. The School paid a capitation fee for using the Daubeny.

20. MCA, SCCM/1/1: 6 Jun. and 24 Oct. 1901.

21. MCA, SCCM/1/2: 2 Mar. 1904.

22. *Ibid.*, 5 Jun. 1910: typed accounts for 1910, 1911 and 1912 attached to the page.

23. *Ibid.*, 18 May, 1 Jun. and 9 Nov. 1910. Some Masters of the School in the nineteenth century had been tough disciplinarians, notably E. R. Christie, whose short tenure (1887/8) saw the roll drop to thirty-six: see Stanier, *Magdalen School* (1958), 169.

24. MCA, SSCM/1/2: 19 Jun. 1912.

25. *Ibid.*, Brownrigg's report, attached to the minutes of 30 Oct. 1912.

26. *Ibid.*, 24 Nov. 1912, 'Report of School Committee' (printed), pp. 7–8. Before the new boarding house, Sherwood had paid the College £240 p.a. for the old one, but the sum had always been restored to him. Once the new boarding house was built, he paid the College £200 p.a. without remission, but Brownrigg had been freed from paying any sum in 1907.

27. *Ibid.*, 'Report', p. 4. This, it was claimed, was why it had been felt necessary to increase their stipend above the sum laid down in the statutes.

28. *Ibid.*, 'Report', p. 9.

29. MCA, SCCM/1/2: 13 and 20 Dec. 1904.

30. MCA, SCCM/1/3: 3 and 12 Jun. 1919; 5 Mar., 30 Apr. and 19 Jul. 1920; 15 Jan. 1921; and 5 May 1922.

31. *Statutes* (1926), sect. xi, no. 1. These statutes also confirmed the College's limited obligations towards Wainfleet and Brackley: *ibid.*, no. 8.

32. Early discussions about what would become Longwall Quadrangle are in MCA, *Acta*, 16 Dec. 1926, 25 May (when the reuse of Buckler's schoolroom is first mentioned), 11 Oct. and 9 Nov. 1927, and 22 Mar. and 23 May 1928; Stanier, *Magdalen School* (1958), 188–91.

PERIOD OF UNCERTAINTY 1928–68

1. Recorded interview, 4 May 2001.

2. White and Darwall-Smith, *The Architectural Drawings of Magdalen College* (2001), 184, and Plate 31.

3. Account of 1928 crisis drawn from Blackwell Papers and Old MCS Club minutes, 1906–36 including the Safeguarding Committee minutes.

4. Board of Education, printed *Report of Inspection of Magdalen College School, Oxford. Held on 8th, 9th and 10th March, 1932*; copy in MCS archive, accompanied by MS letter of congratulation from President Gordon to the Master, 20 May 1932.

5. MCA, BCM/1/4: printed Proceedings of Bursarial Committee, p. 417, 18 Jan. 1937, Report of Sub-Committee on Economy (emphasis added).

6. This school, built 1878–80 to the plans of T. G. Jackson, remained in George Street until transferred in 1966 to Glanville Road in East Oxford where it amalgamated with Southfield School to become Oxford School.

7. The address, which Johnson carefully wrote out and read to avoid misunderstanding, is reproduced in Stanier, *Magdalen School* (1958), App. I, 224–32; cf. 'Commemoration and Prize-Giving', *The Lily*, 15:11 (Jul. 1938), 379–80. The minutes of the Old MCS Club make clear that it was Blackwell who had recruited Johnson, and that the latter's speech was printed at his own cost for wider distribution. *The Lily* was and is the School magazine.

8. Duncan Mackinnon (commoner 1906–10), killed in the Great War, left half his estate, after a life interest to his sister, to the College. The bequest fell in during 1939, when this sister died, and was worth £76,000.

9. MCA, MC:P27/C1/350, 17 Nov. 1938.

10. MCA, MC:VP1/A1/6, fs 103r–105r, with quotation at 105r.

11. *Statutes made for Magdalen College, Oxford, by the University of Oxford Commissioners and by the College under the Universities of Oxford and Cambridge Act, 1923, including all amendments prior to 31st December, 1947* (Oxford, 1947): MS 703/9(b), xi.4 (p. 49). The statute was voted by the required majority in Governing Body on 6 Dec. 1939, and approved by the King in Council on 5 Apr. 1940.

12. Printed Bursarial Committee proceedings 16, 23, and 24 Nov. 1938, 555–59; MCA, MC:P27/C1/350, 17 Nov. 1938, f. 1r–v. For a much later account by another of the Bursar's opponents, J. H. C. Morris, 'The Origin of the Mackinnon Scholarships: College Politics in the Late 1930s', *Magdalen College Record* (1984), 34–38.

13. That Johnson eventually despaired of the College is shown by a copy of a typescript letter from him in the MCS archive, dated 5 Apr. 1944, to Kenneth Wheare (a fellow of University College and an Oxford city councillor), suggesting that the LEA take over the site to run a grammar school.

14. M. Stanier, *Portrait of a Schoolmaster: Robert Spencer Stanier, Master of Magdalen College School, 1944–1967* (Oxford, 1984), 33–37. In a typed letter in the MCS archive dated 7 Nov. 1957, the retired Master, R. Kennard Davis, wrote to Stanier recalling that the war had 'actually brought salvation' to the School, in numbers and in new masters, temporary or permanent, who had signally improved the teaching. Cf. 'School Commemoration and Prize-Giving', *The Lily*, 16:2 (Jul. 1940), 32; and R. S. Stanier, [Report] in 'Commemoration', *The Lily*, 17:2 (Jul. 1945), 13.

15. MCA, CMM/2/4, printed *Acta*, 26 May 1943, CO. 14, and, attached, duplicated 'Notes' by the Master, which incorporated Blackwell's comments.

16. Stanier, *Portrait of a Schoolmaster* (1984), 23–24, 32, 40, and 46–47.

17. MCA, printed *Acta* and papers, esp. for 14 Mar. 1945 and 13 Feb. 1946 (CMM/2/6 and 7); 1946 correspondence between Tizard and Stanier, in MCS archive; MC:VP1/A1/6, f. 142r (P. Johnson, V.-P. 1946 and up to Jun. 1947); R. S. Stanier, [Report] under 'Commemoration', *The Lily*, 17:8 (Jul. 1947), 171–72.

18. Recorded interview, 6 April 2001; R. S. Stanier, 'The Master's Speech', *The Lily*, 21:1 (Sept. 1956), 4.

19. R. S. Stanier, 'The Master's Report', *The Lily*, 18:9 (Sept. 1951), 173.

20. MCA, printed *Acta* and papers, 1 Dec. 1954: CMM/2/15.

21. R. S. Stanier, 'The Master's Speech', *The Lily*, 21:1 (Sept. 1956), 4–5; 'School Notes', *The Lily*, 21:3 (April 1957), 102; R. S. Stanier, 'The Master's

Speech', *The Lily*, 21:4 (Sept. 1957), 141.

22. R. S. Stanier, 'The Master's Speech', *The Lily*, 22:8 (Sept. 1961), 347–49; *idem.*, *The Lily*, 23:3 (Sept. 1962), 102–03; *idem*, *The Lily*, 23:6 (Sept. 1963), 254–56; White and Darwall-Smith, *The Architectural Drawings of Magdalen College* (2001), 212, for plan of new 'Big School', incorporating chapel and hall. See also MCS archive, Appeal Brochure, *Seven Years for Five Centuries* (privately printed at Taunton, undated).

23. R. S. Stanier, 'The Master's Speech', *The Lily*, 21:1 (Sept. 1956), 4; recorded interviews, 4 May 2001, 11 Oct. 2002.

24. Stanier, 'The Master's Speech', *The Lily*, 21:1 (Sept. 1956), 5–6; 'Friends of Magdalen College School', *The Lily*, 22:3 (Jan. 1960), 100–01.

25. Stanier, *Portrait of a Schoolmaster* (1984), 5.

TOWARDS THE PRESENT 1968–2008

1. MCA, CMM/2/31: *Acta*, 19 Jan. 1972, CO.2; MCA, *Acta*, 14 Jun. 1972, CO.11 (ii); accompanying papers. The small subsidy was paid 1969–89.

2. MCA, CMM/2/38: papers 14 Feb. 1979. The Master, Bill Cook, had asked the College for £75,000 to launch the appeal target of £250,000. He cannot have been very pleased with the limited response. School House on the west side of Cowley Place was a boarding house and administrative headquarters.

3. The College agreed to the new arrangement in 1985. See CMM/2/44: papers 13 Feb. 1985. The Company had two members, one the President and Fellows of Magdalen College, the other the Senior Bursar. The Master had wanted the College to establish a completely independent trust for the School.

4. MCA, CCM/2/48: papers 8 Mar. 1989.

5. MCA, CMM/2/57: papers, 11 Oct. and 29 Nov. 1995, esp. 'Magdalen College School, Oxford, Ltd. Long-Term Developments', memo. prepared by the four College governors for the College meeting of 11 Oct. In 1985 the new limited company had been given a ninety-nine year lease, free of rent. Under the new lease, a rent of no more than 4 per cent of the site value is to be paid from 2115.

6. On retirement, one wrote a steamy *roman à clef* in which many stars of the Senior Common Room appeared.

7. Leighfield was chairman of Research Machines, a leading British computer company. For the history of MCS in the 1990s, the author is heavily reliant on his personal recollections as a school governor, and his collection of the School's Governing Body papers.

8. The Colin Sanders Building was named after one of the School's dedicated governors in the 1990s killed in a plane crash, who had made an important contribution to the development of telecommunications.

INDEX